# ENSURING GENERAL WISDOM

---

## THE CRITICAL ROLE NON-EXECUTIVE DIRECTORS AND TRUSTEES PLAY IN EXECUTIVE PERFORMANCE

## J A SUTHERLAND

LAWBOOK CONSULTING LTD T / A LBC WISE COUNSEL

*To my wife and children, thank you for everything.*

## Ensuring General Wisdom

*There is in all ordinary joint stock companies a fixed executive specially skilled, and a somewhat varying council not specially skilled. The fixed manager ensures continuity and experience in the management, and a good board of directors ensures general wisdom.*

— Lombard Street : a description of the money market. Walter Bagehot—1873

# CONTENTS

**WHEN READING NON-EXECUTIVE DIRECTORS (NEDS) PLEASE ALSO READ TRUSTEES OF CHARITIES AND GOVERNORS OF SCHOOLS.**

# FOREWORD

This book came about after I had a punchy conversation with a Non-Executive Director (NED). It was whilst I was working for the UK Parliamentary Commission on Banking Standards. The director took me to task over something I said. That the chief board weakness of the Great Financial Crisis was NEDs failing to challenge and hold executives to account. The director I was talking to asked what my experience was of being a NED. I had to admit very little and before I could say much more he whacked me. He said I had no idea how difficult it is to understand what goes on in a large, complex, modern organisation. In fact it is not difficult it is impossible. He then said that government or regulator attempts to improve governance were doomed. In fact, anyone thinking there is a solution is in cloud cuckoo land.

I heard him out. Then I asked, trying to be helpful, if he needed to improve any aspect of his own knowledge of how banking works? That did not go down well. But, still trying to be helpful, I suggested the NED role had become more demanding and needed more time spent on it. This fell on stony silence. Persevering, I went on to suggest a third option. Had his bank reached such a size and complexity that it had become the impossible job for any NED oversight? Did the bank need simplifying, even to the extent of splitting it up? This third option went down as well as the first two.

With any move to the diplomatic service scuppered I ended with a fourth option, we keep on pretending.

A NED has a difficult job and most people in that role work very hard to live up to the responsibilities. The problem is that point of view, fixing it is impossible. This is not acceptable given the scale of the damage we saw banks inflict.

To say this conversation troubled me puts it mildly and I resolved to get to the bottom of it. Is it beyond fixing? Or, is there a set of solutions out there, even a silver bullet?

My research started with banks but quite soon I found that insurers had the same kind of failings. Wondering if this is a financial services problem took me over to the UK National Health Service (NHS). I researched public inquiries and found failing hospitals exhibiting the same features. To round the research off I had a look at charities, lo and behold, same again.

What do I conclude? Well for a start, it would be wonderful if we could learn from history. Although history itself indicates this is something we don't do well. This excerpt from an inquiry into a NHS failure at Mid Staffs, referencing an earlier NHS failure at Bristol highlights the problem:

*I did feel at least there would be no excuse in future for those responsible to continue to say, after the Bristol report was published ... "with the benefit of hindsight" ... Unhappily, the word "hindsight" occurs at least 123 times in the transcript of the oral hearings of this* [Mid Staffs] *Inquiry, and "benefit of hindsight" 378 times.*[1]

There are 93 references to 'hindsight' in the oral evidence of the Commission I worked for.

Another conclusion is about the importance of the NED role. This silver thread runs through this book from start to finish.

NEDs are part time. They are not always expert in the business of their organisation. But, they have a broad remit to oversee that business and the performance of the full time executives who run it.

Within this broad remit NEDs have two key objectives. Firstly as wise counsel for their executives. NEDs must support and mentor. This is particularly true for CEOs who can experience a very lonely existence.

Secondly though, NEDs have to be able to challenge. To prevent, in the worst case, executive management from capturing the firm for their own ends. This may seem to be a divisive comment, but a prime duty of NEDs is to be a line of defence. One that is able to prevent a toxic self-serving management culture embedding itself. Corporate capture describes executives with no brake on their ability to drive the business in any way they wish. And, by extension, it describes NEDs who should challenge and apply the brake on executives but don't.

The point needs emphasising. Time and again inquiries into corporate failure show executives had captured the business. Even where firms have not failed, capture appears to be at the heart of high pay. How much easier it is to get your executive pay agreed if you have NEDs unable or unwilling to challenge.

Led by a good Chair informed NEDs are the best support executives can have. This support makes organisational and thus personal success more likely. The tragedy is the extent to which some executives do not recognise this. Instead seeing informed NEDs as a form of threat.

Turning to board effectiveness. There is one ultimate measure, the quality of the key decisions the board makes. Which means all the efforts of the Chair of the board need to focus on honing this collective skill. Is this a blindingly obvious statement? Maybe. But if so it still strips out reams of 'corporate governance' material. Material like: board size, diversity, skills mix and time spent. Whilst important these are nonetheless second order issues to decision making quality.

Turning to the structure of this book. It is in two parts which I have styled, in a nod to creativity, The First Part and The Second Part.

If you want to go straight to what it is that NEDs should focus on then dive into The Second Part. However, if you want to understand how organisations fail, and why they fail, then don't leave out The First Part

The First Part strips away jargon and mystery. It describes what banks and insurers are for, how they work, and how they fail.

The Second Part adds the lessons learned from The First Part to its own research. It broadens out into other sectors such as health and charities. It aims at board effectiveness. Uncovering along the way some good practice, best practice and a few sneaky tips. It addresses what NEDs need to do at the nuts and bolts level. In other words, it's five to nine on a rainy Monday morning what, dear NEDs, should you do?

If not a guide about how to avoid disaster it may at least be a map of where the worst elephant traps are. I also pick up on the problem of culture, what it is and what NEDs can do about it.

Who is this book not addressed to? Well, those who fancy easing themselves out of executive life and into retirement in a well paid job. Socially adept timeservers overseeing the activities of equally socially adept executives. This is not something we need. Walter Bagehot writing as long ago as 1873[2] observed the possible damage:

*A large Bank is exactly the place where a vain and shallow person in authority, if he be a man of gravity and method, as such men often are, may do infinite evil in no long time, and before he is detected. If he is lucky enough to begin at a time of expansion in trade, he is nearly sure not to be found out till the time of contraction has arrived, and then very large figures will be required to reckon the evil he has done.*

The last words of this introduction go again to Bagehot but also to super investor Peter Lynch.

Of banking Bagehot wrote:

*The business of banking ought to be simple: if it is hard it is wrong*[3].

Whilst Lynch offers more general business advice:

*The simpler it is, the better I like it. When somebody says, "Any idiot could run this joint," that's a plus as far as I'm concerned, because sooner or later any idiot probably is going to be running it*[4].

1. The Mid Staffordshire NHS Foundation Trust Public Inquiry—Chaired by Robert Francis QC—2013
2. Lombard Street : a description of the money market by Walter Bagehot —1873
3. Ibid.
4. One Up On Wall Street: How To Use What You Already Know To Make Money In The Market—Peter Lynch 1989

# THE FIRST PART—WHERE IT GOES WRONG

# INTRODUCTION

This book takes aim at pretence by stripping away jargon and mystery. It starts by describing what banks are for, how they work, and how they fail. The language is plain and simple.

We learn how ineffective boards contributed to the 2007/8 crisis. That nothing that happened was new suggesting there is every chance it will happen again.

I had a hunch that understanding failure is important. How and why does it happen? Understanding this would lead in turn to understanding what success looks like. Also, why is board effectiveness so elusive?

I went about this by reading many public inquiries into bank failure, some of which go back to the 19th century.

Early on in this endeavour I realised I had no intuitive grasp of why banks go bust. This was in spite of many bank qualifications and a forty plus year banking career. I then found out I am not alone in this respect. Many conversations along this journey showed there are plenty of senior bankers and non-bankers who do not get this either.

The challenge isn't understanding banking, any tyro can grasp that. It's knowing how to cut through the jargon. Wider knowledge of how simple banking is poses rather an embarrassing question. At least to some people. Why are you paid so much?

My observation is not new, as this quote from 'The Bankers New Clothes' reveals:

*The jargon of bankers and banking experts is deliberately impenetrable. This impenetrability helps them confuse policymakers and the public, and it muddles the debate*[1].

The history of bank failures shows how often ineffective governance was the root cause. Another part of that history reveals that banking has had one stand out triumph over very many years. Its success in lobbying politicians. On which point the eminent Andrew Smithers has this to say:

*.....a large industry that produces excessive profits will wish to protect them and will spend money on lobbying politicians to discourage them from introducing measures that enhance competition. This problem is particularly worrying if the industry is subsidised*[2].

This First Part has been for me a bit of a voyage of discovery, during which I have learned a lot and I hope you will too.

---

1. The Bankers' New Clothes: What's Wrong with Banking and What to Do about It by Anat Admati, Martin Hellwig
2. The Road to Recovery: How and Why Economic Policy Must Change by Andrew Smithers

# 1

## WHAT ARE BANKS FOR?

Many banks failed in the Great Financial Crisis. This harmed millions of ordinary people in many different countries. This financial failure sits alongside banks' egregious failures to deal fairly with people. Strong stuff, but true.

That banks have not dealt fairly with people and society at large is in plain evidence. Examples are the LIBOR rate fixing scandal, the mis-sale of payment protection insurance and in the USA sub-prime mortgages. The later revelation that foreign exchange rates were also fixed is more icing on a bitter cake.

Because of the emotion aroused it is easy to forget that banks are an essential part of all economies. Moreover, beyond being essential they should be beneficial. It is worth reflecting a little on 'beneficial banks' and what this means.

Going back to first principles is never a bad thing. In the case of banking a good first principle is Walter Bagehot.'s *Lombard Street*[1]. Writing in 1873 Bagehot explains the benefit of banks to the economy as he knew it then. He pointed to the ability of the British at that time to accumulate diverse small amounts of savings into one place, a bank. And then for the bank to lend these accumulated funds into the economy. Bagehot was quite clear in the competitive advantage this had given Britain:

*A million in the hands of a single banker is a great power: he can at once lend it where he will, and borrowers can come to him, because they know or believe that he has it. But the same sum scattered in tens and fifties through a whole nation is no power at all: no one knows where to find it or whom to ask for it.*

Since Bagehot wrote these words in 1873 finance has changed a great deal. Bagehot's world was that of real cash: gold and silver coins and bullion and it is these sums he saw scattered throughout the land in strongboxes. Placing this treasure in the great safes of banks and getting in return bank notes and the ability to draw more than one had in one's ledger, to overdraw, was his financial world.

In today's global economy banks do not base their ability to lend on bullion and confidence but pretty much on confidence alone.

Banking today is a world away from Bagehot's experiences. Yet he would still recognise the way banks failed in the Great Financial Crisis. He would also understand the damage they can cause when they do.

Whilst this book is not only about banks it will dwell on them in the First Part. We need to try and understand why the same things keep going wrong.

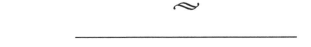

---

1. Lombard Street : a description of the money market by Walter Bagehot —1873

# 2

# HOW BANKS WORK AND HOW THEY FAIL

E arning more on what it lends than it pays on what it borrows is the basis of bank profit. You may want to re-read that sentence. This is the bank business model and always has been.

I know this amounts to a statement of the obvious. But, I am familiar with a building society that charged a big chunk of its borrowers less than it paid its savers. The result was predictable.

Stripping away the myth and jargon means starting with the basics. And so I start with a gripping subject, balance sheets.

A bank balance sheet is not complicated, you can boil it down into the five building blocks shown below. This applies from the tiniest regional bank or credit union to the biggest global bank. These five blocks are your first sign of that myste-rious jargon beginning to slip away.

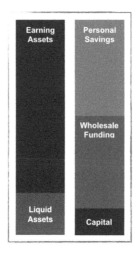

Assets (on the left hand) are either:

- **Liquid** to provide access immediately to cash should there be a demand for repayment of a liability (on the right hand): or

- **Earning** which provide the bank's main income. These earning assets come in all shapes and sizes. They include structured finance, retail mortgages, commercial property lending, investments in companies and government debt. To name but a few.

The bank finances these assets through its liabilities (on the right hand side). Which is to say by obtaining money from third parties. This takes the form of **share capital**, borrowing from the capital markets (**wholesale funding**) and/or from individual savers (**personal savings**). In fact if you re-title liabilities to 'financed by' you have the notion right. The assets are financed by the liabilities.

Management wishing to increase income have four balance sheet strategies. These are covered in later chapters. Unfortunately, each of these strategies increases the fragility of the bank. A fragile bank is prone to failure and banks fail by becoming insolvent or through a liquidity run. The two are often connected. Insolvency is shown below.

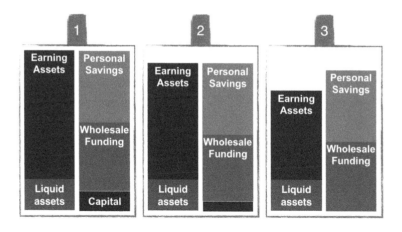

As loan losses occur earning asset values decrease. The balancing item being a reduction of capital on the liabilities side.

If you are at all confused by the concept of capital then imagine the bank at Point *1* above is being closed down. The bank sells its assets on the left hand side for a £ in the £ (to keep things easy) and so the asset side is now all cash. This cash is then repaid to the personal savers and the wholesale lenders. The amount of cash left over equals the dark blue segment and belongs to the shareholders. What is happening at point *2* above is that due to losses, from say bad lending, the assets are worth less. And so if sold will raise less cash. Thus when the savers and wholesale lenders are paid off there is less left for the shareholders. In *3* there isn't even enough to pay off the savers and wholesale lenders and the shareholders have been wiped out.

It is clear from above that the more capital a bank has the better placed it is to absorb losses on its assets. Holding more capital means a bank is much less likely to end up at point *3*. This is important, because at point *3* to prevent personal savers losing money the government has to bail the bank out with taxpayers funds.

Safety dictates banks should hold more capital to minimise

the chance of failure and a taxpayer bail out. Research carried out in the immediate aftermath of the crisis confirmed this:

> *When a financial crisis occurs, we would expect banks with more capital and more stable financing to perform better. We find that this is the case.*[1]

However, regulators' requirements to hold more capital are often met with resistance. The mantra of the day has been that asking banks to 'hold' more capital means they have to keep money back for a rainy day. That holding onto this money prevents the bank from lending into the economy. Despite being wrong this has been promoted many times as accepted wisdom.

The diagram below challenges this wisdom through the balance sheet of one bank. As the bank issues more shares (capital), the bank receives cash in return, (bank moves from Point *1* to Point *2*). The bank will not wish to hold this as cash, on which it earns very little. It will want to convert it into earning assets by, for instance, lending into the economy.

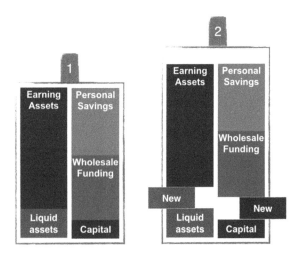

And so a banking myth bites the dust. Increasing the capital of an individual bank far from decreasing its ability to lend into the economy increases it.

Clearly, there is at any point in time a limit to the number of investors wishing to invest capital in banks. There may not be enough if every bank or even the large majority go out capital raising at the same time.

However, the key point to take away is that holding more capital does not prevent an individual bank from lending, quite the reverse.

I hope that now you understand the importance of capital in terms of the safety and soundness of banks.

Additionally, it is not just the fact the bank is more able to absorb losses. It is also that lenders to the bank, especially savvy wholesale lenders, see they are better protected. If you think about it the first losses are always taken by shareholders capital. Losses only reach the wholesale lenders and personal savers once the capital is gone. In the long run higher capital in a bank will also mean a lower cost of funding for the bank. As risk of losses to wholesale lenders lessen, the credit rating of the bank improves. Which should mean the cost of wholesale funding reduces. It being the case that AAA rated debt commands a lower interest rate than BB debt.

This is not to say banks will find raising capital easy. To begin with it may be expensive if the cost of wholesale funding does not decline straightaway. It may also dilute existing shareholders. And, the return on equity (capital) will be harder to achieve because there is more capital to earn a return on.

These three reasons: expense, dilution and lowered return on equity are the likely reasons a bank's executive will not wish to raise more capital. It is just very handy to hide this behind a piece of mystery and jargon. The wrong-headed view that banks holding more capital lend less.

Robert Jenkins, then a member of the Bank of England's

interim Financial Policy Committee, made this point in a speech in September 2012.

> *Has the balance sheet shrunk? No. Has the bank had to cut*
> *credit? No. Does more capital necessarily lead to less lending?*
> *No. ... ... So does society have to choose between safety and*
> *growth? No. But if you fall for this fallacy you will agonise*
> *between doing what is right for the economy short term and*
> *what is right for stability and your country long term. Bankers*
> *have exploited this fear.*"[2]

I said earlier banks fail for two reasons, insolvency where shareholders capital has been wiped out which we have just discussed, and a liquidity run.

Liquidity is in our balance sheets above as 'liquid assets'. The bank can reach for these assets very quickly to repay liabilities. These assets may be cash in the bank's account at the Central Bank or they could be say short dated gilts which the bank can swap for cash without delay.

A run, or liquidity crisis is shown below.

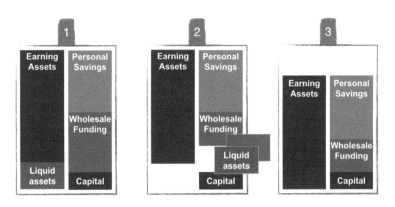

At Point *1* funding can be 're-borrowed' and thus replaced on maturity. At Point *2* the wholesale funding is not renewed on maturity and the bank, finding it cannot replace it from elsewhere has to use its liquid assets to repay the lender of these wholesale funds. At Point *3* the bank has no liquid assets left. The next maturity, personal or wholesale, 'breaks the bank' if it cannot borrow in the market or from the Central Bank as lender of last resort.

There are a few points to bear in mind at this stage:

- Wholesale money, being better informed than personal savers, tends to run first. Northern Rock savers formed queues after wholesale lenders had already begun to 'run' from the bank.
- An illiquid bank is not necessarily insolvent as is clear from point *3* in the figure above.
- Insolvency can take years as bad lending builds up.
- A liquidity crisis can break a bank in days

Fear of insolvency can of itself create a liquidity crisis in the bank. For instance, analysts worrying about hidden losses in a bank's assets may lead to fear that the bank is nearing or actually insolvent. This can lead to wholesale lenders refusing to rollover funding. Thus, fear of insolvency can of itself create a liquidity crisis in a bank.

An example is the failure of Continental Illinois. This was, in 1984, the biggest bank failure in the USA before the 2007/8 crisis. The Chairman of the House inquiry into the failure notes the action of wholesale lenders:

*In the case of Continental, money managers and the foreign investors—about whom we have heard so much—obviously were knowledgeable and spotted problems at the bank. When the regulators failed to force meaningful change, when there was no public announcement or hint of vigorous action to assure the bank's improvement, the investors moved their money. A group clearly more devoted to definitive timely action than our Federal regulators*[3].

As well as showing that wholesale money was well informed notice the criticism of the regulators. A subject we will return to later.

The 2007/8 crisis began with just such a crisis of confidence. Investors and wholesale lenders spotted the growing sub-prime mortgage losses in the USA. But it was unclear which banks had bought into books of these mortgages as part of their earning assets. The wholesale lenders reaction was to stop lending, seek repayment and then sit on the cash. This was of course sensible. The resulting liquidity squeeze on banks proved in too many cases disastrous.

The inquiry into a another bank failure, that of Penn Square Bank in the USA sums up solvency and liquidity:

*As is typical of banks with asset problems, Penn Square suffered from a variety of related ills, including in this case, insufficient capital and liquidity.*[4]

Maybe the shorthand is simply, 'it's the capital stupid'.

In which case you may ask, why is it that bank boards do not get this, why do they not hold higher levels of capital?

Good question, read on!

1. Why Did Some Banks Perform Better During The Credit Crisis?—Andrea Beltratti René M. Stulz—2009
2. https://www.nakedcapitalism.com/2012/09/robert-jenkins-puncturing-bankers-myths.html
3. Inquiry into Continental Illinois Corp. and Continental Illinois National Bank - Hearings before the Subcommittee on Financial Institutions Super-

vision, Regulation and Insurance of The Committee on Banking, Finance and Urban Affairs, House of Representatives - Ninety-Eighth Congress Second Session September 18, 19 And October 4, 1984
4. Penn Square Bank Failure - Hearings Before The Committee On Banking, Finance And Urban Affairs House Of Representatives Ninety-Seventh Congress
    Second Session Part 2 September 29 And 30, 1982

# 3

# IF IT'S THIS SIMPLE WHY DO BANKS FAIL?

There may be two reasons and these may be combined. The pay of executive management could encourage taking risks that threaten and weaken capital and liquidity as discussed above and NEDs could be unable or unwilling to challenge.

An example would be not recognising bad lending promptly. When management recognise bad debts they do this through reduced profits, or even losses, and have to write down earning assets and thus see the capital of the bank reduce. If however they can convince the outside world and the NEDs that loans are really performing, or will perform, or they extend forbearance to the borrower to make it look like the loan is performing, then the value of the asset is not reduced and so the amount of capital looks better than it really is.

Bagehot saw this as clearly in his day as we see it today:

*Every great crisis reveals the excessive speculations of many houses which no one before suspected.*[1]

This takes us back to the market's confidence in the bank. As soon as analysts suspect a problem with asset valuations then wholesale lenders will start to demand repayment on maturity and if they do rollover only do so for much shorter periods. Thus the bank edges towards the entrance to the banking doom loop.

This may sound idiotic: leave alone why would the NEDs allow this, why would the executive do this? Surely everyone would have a natural incentive to guard the safety and security of the bank through the business cycle, through good times and bad.

A powerful reason has been the market's demand for executive incentives to be aligned with those of the shareholders, the owners of the capital in the bank balance sheet. On the face of it the simplest way is to reward management for increasing the return on equity which is what shareholders want. This leads to lots of executive share options and bonuses that pay out on the share price increasing. What could possibly go wrong?

The dichotomy between return and fragility is explained below. Here we have two banks each with a total balance sheet size of £11 billion from which they are both generating annual profits of £110 million. Bank A is funded with £1 billion of capital, Bank B with £3 billion of capital.

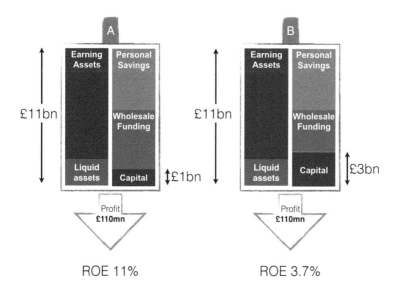

The return on equity calculation, in our example profit divided by capital, gives the game away. Bank B is a much safer institution because it has a bigger first loss buffer, having more capital. However, the return on equity is two thirds less than if it were capitalised only to the extent of £1 billion as Bank A is.

If Bank B reflects an ambition for a bank to be better capitalised, and thus more able to weather the business cycle, it is rational for a management team incentivised to maximise return on equity to resist this. It is equally rational for shareholders to sell Bank B and buy Bank A, putting pressure on the share price of Bank B and thus pressure on its board to improve 'results'.

The incentivisation of executives in line with shareholder expectations or shareholder value started, according to Roger Martin, with a 1976 paper by Professor Michael Jensen and Dean William Meckling of the University of Rochester. Jensen and Meckling argued that a key principal-agent problem needed correcting:

> *The principal-agent problem occurs, the article argued, because agents have an inherent incentive to optimise activities and resources for themselves rather than for their principals. Ignoring Peter Drucker's foundational insight of 1973 that the only valid purpose of a firm is to create a customer, Jensen and Meckling argued that the singular goal of a company should be to maximise the return to shareholders[2].*

The exhortation to increase shareholder value has undoubtedly blind sided many boards:

> *To achieve that goal, the academics argued, the company should give executives a compelling reason to place shareholder value maximisation ahead of their own nest-feathering. Unfortunately, as often happens with bad ideas that*

*make some people a lot of money, the idea caught on and has even become the conventional wisdom*[3].

This concentration on the shareholder as the only stakeholder can place a great strain on safe and sound management of businesses, but most especially banks. It also ignores the direction of the UK Companies Act[4] which is very clear, as shown below, on the wide range of stakeholders Directors must have regard to.

*A director of a company must act in the way he considers, in good faith, would be most likely to promote the success of the company for the benefit of its members as a whole, and in doing so have regard (amongst other matters) to—*

*a) the likely consequences of any decision in the long term,*

*b) the interests of the company's employees,*

*c) the need to foster the company's business relationships with suppliers, customers and others,*

*d) the impact of the company's operations on the community and the environment,*

*e) the desirability of the company maintaining a reputation for high standards of business conduct, and*

*f) the need to act fairly as between members of the company.*

This companies act direction has at long last found support in the UK Corporate Governance Code 2018, which now requires a report on how all of the stakeholder interests have been considered.

In his 2012 report John Kay noted this about the definition of shareholder value that:

*This definition cannot be equated with a responsibility to maximise the current share price, although we received evidence that some company directors thought that it could.*[5]

We will take a further look at incentives in the Second Part but for now it is enough to say that incentivising return on equity has toxic possibilities when the incentives are aimed at executives. In the case of the failure of HBoS the incentives went beyond even the executives and were found to extend to the non-executive Chair, about which the Parliamentary Commission on Banking Standards had this to say:

> *HBoS NED independence was also compromised by a Chair who was himself incentivised with share options. The Chair is crucial in providing leadership and enabling NEDs to challenge, sharing the incentive to increase ROE dilutes the challenge considerably.*[6]

1. Lombard Street : a description of the money market by Walter Bagehot —1873
2. Roger L. Martin: Fixing the Game: Bubbles, Crashes, and What Capitalism Can Learn from the NFL.
3. Ibid.
4. Companies Act 2006
5. The Kay Review Of UK Equity Markets And Long-Term Decision Making—Final Report July 2012
6. House of Lords House of Commons Parliamentary Commission on Banking Standards 'An accident waiting to happen': The failure of HBOS Fourth Report of Session 2012-13

# 4

# ROBUST OR FRAGILE

I mentioned earlier the idea that banks could become more fragile as a drive to increase income takes place. This is how it happens.

Each of the five blocks in the bank balance sheet can either be robust or fragile. The job of the bank's board and its regulator is to understand how blocks can go from being robust to fragile and what the impact on the health of the bank is likely to be.

There are four strategies within the balance sheet which increase income. These are numbered in the figure below. Each is open to abuse.

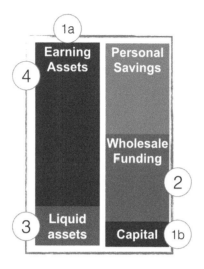

**Balance sheet strategies**

1. Leverage—total of capital 1b as a proportion of total assets (earning assets plus liquidity) 1a
2. Short funding maturity
3. Poor liquidity buffer, amount and/or quality
4. High risk earning assets/misjudging risk/misjudging valuation

**1 - Leverage**—the simple mathematics of the assets earning more than the liabilities cost means there is a natural incentive to increase the size of the bank's balance sheet by borrowing more from savers or through wholesale funding. The bigger the balance sheet the bigger the absolute value of the margin which in turn increases the return on capital, capital not being increased. This all looks great from the shareholders point of view, return on equity increases, no doubt so does the share price, what could possibly go wrong?

Well, remember that capital absorbs losses in the assets as these losses are incurred. If capital starts off as 6% of the total value of all assets, then the bank has to see its assets written down by 6% before it becomes insolvent. If the bank borrows more personal savings and/or wholesale funding to double its assets size then the capital is only 3% of the total value of the assets and thus a much smaller percentage loss results in insolvency. The bank is more fragile.

**2 - Short maturity of funding**—increasing leverage increases funding costs because there is more funding on which the bank has to pay interest. Keeping maturities short is a cheaper form of funding than longer term maturities simply due to the shape of the yield curve, it is usually cheaper to borrow for a week than for a year. The problem is that if all of the funding is at one-week maturity then the bank is always one week away from a liquidity crisis. This is simply because if the lenders of wholesale have doubts about either the bank itself or the financial markets generally they will stop lending. If all of a bank's funding maturities are due within a week this is a quick-fire route to disaster. Whereas, if 1% are due in a week, 5% in a month, 10% in a quarter etc the bank has more time to batten down the hatches.

Shortening the maturity of funding reduces the cost of the liabilities and whilst this increases the margin, profit and RoE it also makes the bank more fragile.

**3 - Poor liquidity buffer**—liquid assets, near cash, generate little income for the bank and thus have an opportunity cost. This tempts management to invest instead in better returning but illiquid assets. Having earning assets doing double duty as liquid assets is a dangerous pretence.

You might imagine the conversation:

*"We're only earning ⅛% on those short term treasuries in our liquidity pool" … …*

*"You're right and do you know we haven't had a run in 130 years, surely this is too much liquidity, the risk is very low"*

*... ...*

*"Hmm, I see your point, that high yielding sovereign debt is earning 11%, bargain!".*

Illiquid assets mean what they say. At the point the bank, under stress, needs cash it may well find the sovereign debt saleable only at a massive discount, or even totally unsaleable.

During 2006 a number of small building societies were attracted to higher rates they could earn on their liquidity pool. Unfortunately, the banks they deposited their cash with were in Iceland. When those banks collapsed in the Great Financial Crisis the building societies discovered their Icelandic liquid assets were literally frozen, causing several to fail.

**4 - High risk assets**—higher risk drives higher returns. In other words the reason a lender can for example charge more interest for sub prime mortgages is that over the cycle more sub prime borrowers default, the extra interest earnings being needed to pay for these extra losses. The management team wanting to boost profits in the short term will lend to such as sub prime mortgages, and so in the short term the assets earn more. This is great, especially if the management team can bale out with a bonus before the losses come in. Of course in the medium to long term more risk has been built into the balance sheet, the bank is more fragile.

These four strategies, or if they happen unbeknownst, failings, are at the heart of all bank collapses since time immemorial. The later chapter on the history of bank failures confirms this, evidencing cases from the 19th century to today. Further evidence is provided by one of the conclusions of the US commission into the financial crisis of 2007/8:

*High leverage, inadequate capital, and short-term funding*

*made many financial institutions extraordinarily vulnerable to*
*the downturn in the market in 2007. The investment banks had*
*leverage ratios, by one measure, of up to 40 to 1. This means*
*that for every $40 of assets, they held only $1 of capital.*[1]

That high returns can be an indicator of future losses is
shown from the research of Beltratti and Stulz in 2009:

*One striking result is that banks with the highest returns in*
*2006 had the worst returns during the crisis. More specifically,*
*the banks in the worst quartile of performance during the crisis*
*had an average return of -87.44% during the crisis but an*
*average return of 33.07% in 2006. In contrast, the best-*
*performing banks during the crisis had an average return of*
*-16.58% but they had an average return of 7.80% in 2006.*[2]

And, if we want to find one poster child for bank failure then
Lehman Brothers is now surely it:

*But the assets were predominantly long–term, while the*
*liabilities were largely short–term. Lehman funded itself*
*through the short–term repo markets and had to borrow tens or*
*hundreds of billions of dollars in those markets each day from*
*counter-parties to be able to open for business. Confidence was*
*critical. The moment that repo counter-parties were to lose*
*confidence in Lehman and decline to roll over its daily funding,*
*Lehman would be unable to fund itself and continue to*
*operate……In 2006, Lehman made the deliberate decision to*
*embark upon an aggressive growth strategy, to take on*
*significantly greater risk, and to substantially increase*
*leverage on its capital*[3].

There is a fifth reason for bank failure, and that is rogue trad-
er/fraud. Whilst this kind of loss might seem unavoidable it is

likely to be a self-inflicted failure of risk oversight and controls. The fraud which led to the demise of Barings bank in 1995 is a classic:

> "*Although Leeson's control over back office operations explains how he was able to initiate the fraud, weaknesses in internal and external oversight explain how the fraud escaped detection over so long a period*".[4]

Contrary to perceived wisdom Leeson did not cause Barings to fail it was Barings that caused Barings to fail. The lack of effective supervision, controls and independent audit allowing Leeson to operate as he did.

A typical failing of all boards is to examine failures such as loan losses and trading losses but not to examine success. The inability to look through the huge profits at Barings, as reported by Leeson, and failing to ask the question 'why are we making so much money here?' is not unusual. Better yet of course would have been the Barings board asking: "if we are making so much profit in the Far East why are we continually sending funds there?" Barings is a good example of where a healthy dose of scepticism was replaced by celebration:

> But his profitability was "*regarded with admiration rather than scepticism*".[5].

Failing to look through 'super-profits' is all the more inexplicable given the well understood relationship between risk and reward, more reward must mean that somewhere there is more risk.

1. Final Report Of The National Commission On The Causes Of The Financial And Economic Crisis In The United States Submitted By The Financial Crisis Inquiry Commission Pursuant to Public Law 111-21 January 2011
2. Why Did Some Banks Perform Better During The Credit Crisis?—Andrea Beltratti René M.—2009
3. United States Bankruptcy Court Southern District Of New York Lehman Brothers Holdings Inc.,
      March 11, 2010 Report Of Anton R. Valukas, Examiner
4. BCCI & Barings: Bank Resolutions Complicated by Fraud and Global Corporate Structure
      by Richard J. Herring
5. Ibid.

# SHARE BUY BACKS ARE A GOOD THING FOR SOME

W e have seen the havoc that can be wrought on a bank by asset losses which deplete capital. We have also seen that raising capital in the market is one way to replenish capital and strengthen the balance sheet and thus the bank. However, going to the market has its drawbacks. Existing shareholders may not wish to invest further in the bank nor welcome the dilution of their share of the bank by the arrival of new shareholders. Also, if the bank is seen to be raising capital at a point when it is stressed then the share price will be depressed, and if the share price is depressed then the shares sold will raise less capital for the bank.

The far better solution beyond obviously avoiding asset losses is to retain profits in the business, retained profits increase capital. Unfortunately, a self-serving bonus culture resting on return on equity and encouraging an increase in share prices dictates that executives will prefer to pay out dividends or buy back shares. High dividends make shares more attractive, but that also means profit is not being retained in the business and thus capital is not being bolstered.

Share buy-backs are dealt with in the Second Part of this

book when we consider financial incentives in more detail. Suffice to say at this point executives incentivised via the share price cannot help but notice that if the number of shares in issue is reduced the price tends to go up. This is simply because of the mathematics of RoE: if E is reduced by share buy back but R is maintained then this inflates the RoE. All good consequences follow: the share price, plaudits for the executives and the value of their bonuses.

A key decision for the board, when considering the capital strength of the bank, is how to split profits. There are four options which are not mutually exclusive:

1. Pay dividends to shareholders
2. Buy-back shares
3. Invest the profit in the business e.g. capital projects such as IT, premises or simply using it to finance lending etc
4. Pay out to staff

This debate within the board is crucial. Deciding between the four options means striking a balance between shareholders who may want the maximum dividend possible, versus strengthening the balance sheet by building up capital or investing in the future of the business and paying well to attract and retain high quality staff.

∾

# 6

# TOO BIG TO FAIL, WHAT IS THIS ALL ABOUT?

The phrase too big to fail was first coined by Senator McKinney of Connecticut during the Federal inquiry into the failure of Continental Illinois National Bank (CINB) in 1984.

*Mr. Chair, let us not bandy words. We have a new kind of bank. It is called too big to fail. TBTF, and it is a wonderful bank[1].*

CINB was the biggest bank failure in the USA prior to the banking crisis of 2007/8 and followed a period of strengthened US bank regulation. This combination: a huge bank failure, new regulation and the perceived failure of the regulators led to some pretty blunt words from Senator St Germain of Rhode Island, Chair of the inquiry:

*In 1977 and 1978, we battled uphill against the combined bank and regulatory lobby to enact an entire set of new and improved supervisory powers—to make certain that no one in the Federal supervisory bureaucracy could claim they lacked the tools.*

*Yet, today, we return to this forum faced with what is, for all* *practical purposes, the granddaddy of bank failures, a $44 billion money centre bank that rolled into the ditch uncontrolled by its $500,000-a-year Chair and the rest of the megabucks management team—or the Federal bank supervisory system*[2].

CINB was brought down by a wholesale funding run borne out of market concerns that losses were not truly reflected in the valuations of earning assets in its balance sheet. Once the bank had been taken over by the authorities the true horror of the losses was revealed and the market rumours and fears of insolvency were confirmed.

Too big to fail (TBTF) became the description for CINB because the US regulatory authorities shied away from inflicting losses on personal savers and wholesale funders. This was because of the perceived impact this would have in confidence and on the economy. CINB was in fact an object example of Figure 2 above where we saw earning asset losses wiping out capital. Government would then have to step in with funding, or else retail savers and wholesale funders would lose money.

TBTF is shown in the figure below.

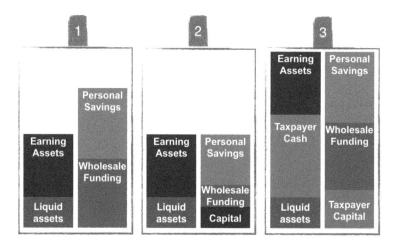

At Point 1 we see a bank that has sustained such losses that shareholders have been wiped out and where total assets when sold will not be sufficient to repay what is owed to wholesale lenders and retail savers. At Point 2 we see the bank recapitalised by converting the wholesale debt to shares at less than £1 for a £ and the personal savers losing part of their deposits. Point 2 is a bank that is not too big to fail, it has failed and its savings customers and lenders have taken losses. The original share-holders having been wiped out and the new shareholders are the wholesale lenders from point 1.

In the case of CINB the regulatory authorities appear to have decided that, due to the size of the bank, inflicting extensive losses on personal savers as described at Point 2 would be a dangerous move potentially impacting confidence in banks across the USA. Therefore, as shown in Point 3 above, taxpayer dollars were pumped into the bank when it was at at Point 1 to the extent that capital was built up. In this way retail savers and wholesale lenders suffered no losses. CINB was indeed too big to fail.

Prior to CINB, bank failures had led to losses being taken by savers above the deposit guarantee limit and by providers of wholesale funding. There is ample evidence from the US of the 1920s of thousands of small banks failing and savers losing money in the process, there being little or no deposit insurance at that time.

After the CINB failure in 1984 the market noticed TBTF: credit rating agencies and lenders of wholesale funding came to realise that when a bank fails then lenders of wholesale funding would not after all be expected to absorb losses. In effect the loans they were making to the banks were guaranteed by the taxpayer. This led to a reduction in the price of such lending to banks, which led to banks taking more of this lending, which led to the proportion of capital to total assets falling and leverage increasing. This in turn led to ROE increasing, share prices increasing and those bonuses linked to ROE and share prices paying out. All bank Christmases arrived at once.

While failure is a feature of all forms of business activity, the discipline of the marketplace—the fear of the consequences of failure—tends to reduce the extent of recklessness, at least among the management of major corporations. In banking, this market discipline has been very much weaker, thanks to what is effectively the taxpayer guarantee.

This weakness of market discipline led at least in part to the high leverage of banks in the run up to the 2007/8 crisis. Many banks went into 2007 with leverage ratios, capital divided by total assets, of less than 2%. In other words a slight puff of wind, resulting in 1 to 2% of loans defaulting would wipe out the capital of the bank, rendering it insolvent. This however was OK, because the taxpayer would pick up the bill, the very essence of TBTF.

The failures in the UK of HBoS, RBS and Northern Rock simply reinforced this idea of a taxpayer guarantee. The queues outside the branches of Northern Rock in 2007 were of savers who suddenly realised they didn't know how the deposit guarantee worked, or indeed if it would be honoured. In the end after only a few days of 24 hour news flashing these queues around the world the UK government promised to guarantee all deposits even those above the deposit guarantee. This was then trumped by the Irish government who not only guaranteed all savers deposits but also all wholesale funding. Truly, TBTF had come of age.

TBTF is central to the problems in the banking industry: it effectively reduces moral hazard as bank boards, shareholders, wholesale markets and personal savers find themselves protected by the taxpayer from the consequences of risks being run in the bank.

TBTF is however not just about the taxpayer guaranteeing bank liabilities. It is also about the fear of the unknown, not knowing what the impact of a big failure on economies and thus society will be. The collapse of Lehman's in 2008 showed how interconnected banks had become and also how poor they could be at record keeping. It quickly became apparent that many of the thousands of contracts Lehman had entered into were not well documented or not documented at all. This meant it was not clear which part of Lehman's was involved in individual deals and the total risks were simply unknown.

*And just a month before Lehman's collapse, the Federal Reserve Bank of New York was still seeking information on the exposures created by Lehman's more than 900,000 derivatives contracts*[3].

Regulators today are cooperating internationally to find a way of measuring interconnectedness between different parts of the global financial markets. The intention being to make sure balance sheets are strong enough to take account of losses that may arise if another organisation fails.

A further complication is that of critical economic functions (CEFs), this being the Bank of England description for such things as payment and settlement systems. If a bank fails and it provides current accounts for instance, are those current accounts to be frozen pending a payout from the deposit guarantee? How will households and businesses cope if they suddenly have no current account? If they had agreed an overdraft with the failed bank, how easy will it be to reinstate this with a new bank, especially if the new bank is being extra cautious because of the failure of one of its brethren?

1. Senator Stewart B McKinney - Inquiry Into Continental Illinois Corp. And

Continental Illinois National Bank Tuesday, September 18, 1984 House Of Representatives, Subcommittee On Financial Institutions Supervision, Regulation And Insurance, Committee On Banking, Finance And Urban Affairs,

2. Inquiry Into Continental Illinois Corp. And Continental Illinois National Bank Tuesday, September 18, 1984 House Of Representatives, Subcommittee On Financial Institutions Supervision, Regulation And Insurance, Committee On Banking, Finance And Urban Affairs,

3. Final Report Of The National Commission On The Causes Of The Financial And Economic Crisis In The United States Submitted By The Financial Crisis Inquiry Commission -21 January 2011

# 7

# HAS THIS EVER HAPPENED BEFORE?

T he short answer is yes. In 2008 banks did not fail for new reasons, this has happened many times before.

My research has included contemporary failures such as Northern Rock. I was also drawn to the excellent work of the team that produced: "An Accident Waiting to Happen" recording the downfall of HBoS. But, I also strayed back into the early 20th and late 19th centuries. US congressional inquiries (1907, 1908, 1913, 1931, 1933 and 1985) and other US and UK bank failures from 1860 to the present day.

I also looked at insurance failures such as HIH in Australia and Equitable in the UK. And finally, to the National Health Service and in the charity sector, Kids Company.

The research reveals *characteristics* of failure and *causes* of how these come about.

For banks, there appear to have been five common *characteristics* of failure and three underlying *causes*. The *characteristics* of a failing hospital (poor care, poor hygiene, over stretched expert staff) may be different to a bank or insurer, but I find the *causes* are the same.

The first five failure *characteristics* of banks I found are:

high leverage, short funding maturity, poor liquidity, poor risk assets and rogue trader/fraud. Later research revealed two more.

One is miss-selling, which caused the failure of the Norwich & Peterborough Building Society. The regulator found its sale of complex savings products too sophisticated for the customers who invested. The redress costs, putting the customers back to where they would have been had they not invested, cost £51mn and proved too heavy a burden.

> *Following discussions with the regulatory community, including the FSA, N&P has agreed voluntarily to make ex gratia payments to all customers ... These payments will cost N&P a total of approximately £51m.*[1]

Although yet to cause a failure cyber is the second. This may take the form of an attack, state or criminally sponsored, or be an operational failure. It was the latter that nearly brought down the RBS Group in the summer of 2012. For several weeks RBS and its NatWest and Ulster Bank subsidiaries were unable to make and receive payments on behalf of customers. This was due to a straightforward software update going wrong.

The three *causes* of failure are: poor incentives, poor governance and poor risk management. But, I can be more focused by inviting you to think why incentives and risk management might be poor. Would this be through excellent governance? Obviously not, so I consider poor governance to be the pre-eminent cause. The Second Part of this book reveals that corporate leadership is a better description than governance. It is the way boards influence not only financial results but the culture of the business and the way its workforce conduct themselves.

Depressingly, neither *characteristics* nor *causes* are novel, this has been happening to banks for centuries. And I only include the 19th, 20th and 21st centuries here. Any historian which I am not will volunteer many more examples.

The strength and persistence of bank's political lobbying is a long-term feature. For 100 years US banks have tried and sometimes succeeded in resisting the separation of investment and commercial banking. The contemporary debate about separating investment and commercial banking is not new.

A recent example of lobbying includes US banks trying to dilute the Volcker rule and banks generally trying to avoid leverage ratios. The 'if you make us hold more capital we will have less to lend' myth.

*Characteristics, causes* and banks' lobbying have been consistent through the years. Thus the key leadership challenge is how to use 'corporate memory' to mitigate the risk of failure. The 'hindsight' quote from the hospital failure shows this is not only a banking problem.

To test out this theory of *characteristics*, *causes* and corporate memory let us now take a journey through banking history.

---

1. FSA Final Notice 15 April 2011—to Norwich and Peterborough Building Society—2.6 A p4

# 8

# BANKING AND FINANCIAL CRISES

F inancial crises involve some need for government policy intervention due to the serious impact on the economic health of the country. The distinction, in bank terms, is between a single bank in distress and the feature of financial crises which is 'waves' of banks in distress. The irony is that whilst getting out of a financial crisis has often involved government intervention, getting into it in the first place was also probably government inspired.

The eminent American academic Charles Calomiris[1] distinguishes between failures (insolvency) and panics (liquidity runs) and goes on to identify government as a cause:

> "*Risk-inviting microeconomic rules of the banking game that are established by government have always been the key additional necessary condition to producing a propensity for banking distress, whether in the form of a high propensity for banking panics or a high propensity for waves of bank failures*".

The largest wave of bank failures occurred in the US in the 1920s, and evidence here is found of government intervention:

*The large wave of failures in the 1920s were of small rural banks that had been enabled by government to fund themselves with tax exempt bonds, the banks then lent into an already inflated farming market. The assets* [farm mortgages] *appeared good lending but as the bubble collapsed not only were these found to be high-risk loss making assets but also that the bonds, at shorter maturities than the mortgages, created liquidity crises.*[2]

If you're a bit uncertain about 'tax exempt bonds', they were simply a form of retail saving.

Ninety years later, repeating the voices of history, we find government influence again at work:

*Clinton set the wheels in motion: Bush did little to stop the juggernaut ... of course, many of the banks played their part as well, but the prime responsibility is a political one of seeking to increase home ownership at any price.*[3]

The argument is not that government interference is the only cause of banks' stress and failure, but that widespread failure or stress of many banks in "waves", is frequently a government inspired phenomenon.

An example of government interference is the emergence of deposit insurance in the US. In the nineteenth and early twentieth century several US states enacted deposit insurance, which has enabled researchers to measure performance of non-insured states against insured states:

*"Other things equal, state banks in states with guaranty funds*

*failed at a higher rate than state banks in states without guaranty funds".*[4]

The underlying reason appears to have been the lack of moral hazard in the deposit insured states. In states where deposit insurance was not provided savers would pay much closer attention to the strength or otherwise of the banks. Knowing this management were also more inclined to pay attention to strength in terms of both liquidity and capital, moral hazard in action.

Deposit insurance eventually passed into Federal law via Glass-Steagall but did so against the wishes of President Roosevelt and Senator Glass.

*Deposit insurance was seen by opponents as an undesirable special interest legislation designed to benefit small banks. Roosevelt, Glass, and others acquiesced for practical political reasons, to get other legislation passed, not because they wanted deposit insurance. Bad economics is sometimes good politics.*[5]

On Glass-Steagall Calomiris has this observation:

*For Henry Steagall, the Depression offered the chance to pass a long dormant proposal for federal deposit insurance (which had been understood for fifty years to be special interest legislation for small agricultural banks). For Carter Glass, the Depression provided the opportunity to push through his decades-long quest to separate commercial banks from capital markets by fostering the now discredited view that the mixing of commercial and investment banking had caused banks to collapse during the Depression.*[6]

Today the impact on moral hazard of deposit insurance is

better understood. The experience of the 2007-2008 crisis that the deposit guarantee limit created in 'peacetime' is, in times of crisis, prone to suspension by government. However, any impression that the guarantee is in effect without limit has been offset by regulators requiring much higher levels of capital and liquidity.

Between 1850 and 1930 there were many more banking failures and crises in the USA than in the UK. Behind this difference appear to be two root causes: an effective central bank and 'unit banking'.[7]

The Bank of England was established in 1694 but it was not until the late 19th century that it could be said to be an effective influence on the stability of the British banking system. Through experience it clarified its role of lender of last resort and developed its role with an eye on the hazard it could cause to the financial system by its own actions.

The distinguished historian Forrest Capie observes:

*A well-behaved bank could fail through no fault of its own if a shock hit the system and a panic developed. That should not happen with a proper lender of last resort in place. And indeed the understanding of that was a major factor in crises being avoided in England.*[8]

In contrast the US experienced numerous panics and failures. With two abortive attempts at creating a central bank in the nineteenth century it had to wait until 1913 for the establishment of its central bank in the shape of the Federal Reserve System. In addition the US was hampered by widespread unit banking whereas the UK had fewer, larger, multiple branched banks.

The unit banking model was enshrined in US law whereby banks were not allowed to branch across state lines, and in some states were severely restricted within the state. In the twentieth century this was behind much of the international expansion of

US banks who finding growth in their home markets restricted looked to overseas markets instead.

Jones and Angley[9] refer to the extent of unit banking when discussing the thousands of US bank failures during the 1920s:

> *Nearly all the banks that went broke during the ten boom years of the twenties were small.   Only 12% had a capitalisation above $100,000 and 40% were village establishments started with less than $25,000.   Most of these never should have been opened, for the capital investments were too small.*

Also by evidence to Senator Glass Chairing sub-committee hearings in 1931 the Comptroller of Currency said:

> *'Well, 90% of the* [failed] *banks are in small rural communities.  Economic changes have put these small communities within easy distances of the larger commercial centres where the banks are stronger and more efficient in every respect, and as a consequence of this ready access to those centres, the cream of the banking business has gone to those centres, which has had the effect of reducing the opportunities of the small country banks to such an extent that they find it difficult to earn a sufficient amount of money to charge off their losses and to pay a reasonable dividend, and neither can they offer anything like the facilities which the city bank can offer, and with these opportunities removed, the bank is not able to maintain itself'.*[10]

Mapping the characteristics against just a few of the many bank failures from the late 19th century forwards we can see in the table below some banks failing for idiosyncratic reasons whilst others went down in waves.

| Firm | High Leverage | Short Funding | Poor Liquidity | High Risk Assets | Rogue Trader Fraud | Miss-selling | Single, or part of a Wave |
|---|---|---|---|---|---|---|---|
| 1866 Overend Gurney | X | | | X | X | | Single |
| 1878 City of Glasgow | | | | | X | | Single |
| 1890 Barings | | | | X | | | Single |
| 1932 Continental Illinois | X | X | X | X | | | Wave |
| 1932 Guardian Trust Co | X | X | X | X | X | | Wave |
| 1982 Penn Square Bank | X | X | X | X | | | Single |
| 1984 Continental Illinois | X | X | X | X | | | Single |
| 1995 Barings | | | | | X | | Single |
| 2007 Northern Rock | X | X | X | X | | | Wave |
| 2008 RBS | X | X | X | X | | | Wave |
| 2008 Dunfermline BSoc | | | | X | | | Wave |
| 2008 HBoS | X | X | X | X | | | Wave |
| 2008 Washington Mutual | | X | X | X | | | Wave |
| 2008 Lehman Brothers | X | X | X | X | Repo 105/108 | | Wave |
| 2011 Norwich & Peterborough BSoc | | | | | | X | Single |

I have used the word depressing once before, it is worth using it again, by drawing your attention to the similarities in this table of only a selected group of bank failures over roughly 145 years.

You may also notice that Barings had been rescued in 1890 before its final failure 105 years later and that Continental Illinois, in similar fashion, was rescued in 1932 before its final demise in 1984.

---

1. Banking Crises and the Rules of the Game, Calomiris October 2009
    •A 'panic' is a failure of confidence in a bank, causing a run on its deposits and forcing it to close its doors. Subsequently, the sale of the bank's assets may well pay back all savers deposits and even return a dividend to share holders. The bank being a victim of holding illiquid assets it could not turn into cash fast enough to repay depositors.
    •A 'failure' is synonymous with insolvency: the bank taking losses on its assets sufficient to wipe out the shareholders and potentially some or all of the depositors.
2. Why do Banks Fail? Evidence from the 1920s, Alston, Grove and Wheelock 1994

3. Fannie Mae and Freddie Mac – Turning the American Dream into a Nightmare

4. Deposit Insurance: A History Of Failure *Thies and Gerlowski* h*ttp://www.-cato.org/sites/cato.org/files/serials/files/cato-journal/1989/1/cj8n3-8.pdf*

5. Banking crises and the rules of the game—Calomiris October 2009

6. How to restructure failed banking systems: lessons from the U.S. in the 1930's and Japan in the 1990's Charles W. Calomiris Joseph R. Mason April 2003

7. A unit bank is a bank with only one branch, and thus distinguished from any bank with two or more branches known as a branched bank.

8. Professor Forrest Capie, written evidence to the Parliamentary Commission on Banking Standards 2013, ev1512

9. Fifty Billion Dollars – The History of the Reconstruction Finance Corporation, J H Jones and E Angley

10. Hearings Before A Subcommittee Of The Committee On Banking And Currency United States Senate Seventy-First Congress Third Session Pursuant To S. Res. 71 A Resolution To Make A Complete Survey Of The National And Federal Reserve Banking Systems—Part 1 January 1931

# CAUSES

The *causes* through which these *characteristics* emerge are a short list:

1. Incentives
2. Governance
3. Risk management.

**Incentives**
The potential for incentives to create problems emerged in written evidence to the Parliamentary Commission in 2012:

> *Bankers are responsive to, and largely remunerated in the same way as, shareholders ... Given the incentives to raise the return on equity by increasing leverage, the surprise is perhaps that it took them so long to do so.*[1]

This incentive structure also encourages non-productive behaviour designed to flatter profits. The exploitation of accounting rules is an example. A prescient article in Bloomberg Businessweek in 2006 revealed how banks were booking to profit interest they had not actually received. Borrowers on Adjustable Rate Mortgages (ARMs) who were not even covering interest, let alone repaying the principal, were treated by the lending bank as though they had paid the interest in full for accounting purposes:

*For many industries, so-called accrual accounting, which lets companies book sales when they contract for them rather than when they receive the cash, makes sense. The revenues will eventually come. But accrual accounting doesn't apply well to option Adjustable Rate Mortgages (ARMs), since it's more difficult to know if unpaid interest will ever cross a banker's desk.*[2]

An example is illustrated by Kirsten Grind in her record of the failure of Washington Mutual (WaMu):

*At the end of 2005, nearly half of the loans in WaMu's $70 billion Option ARM portfolio were negatively amortising. WaMu customers had avoided paying $316 million in interest, up from just $19 million a year earlier. WaMu booked that interest as earnings, which meant that the bank, in accordance with national accounting standards, was making money off of borrowers not paying down their debt.*[3]

In hindsight, the perverse incentive whereby bank executives would be paid cash bonuses on 'profit' made this kind of exploitation of accounting rules fairly predictable. The main inquiry in the United States into the 2007/8 crisis also identified this problem:

*Compensation systems—designed in an environment of cheap money, intense competition, and light regulation—too often rewarded the quick deal, the short-term gain—without proper*

*consideration of long-term consequences. Often, those systems*
*encouraged the big bet—where the payoff on the upside could*
*be huge and the downside limited. This was the case up and*
*down the line—from the corporate boardroom to the mortgage*
*broker on the street*[4].

I take some issue with this comment, because *cheap money,*
*intense competition, and light regulation* might have been characteristics of the environment but they were not the cause
whereby these schemes were engineered by executives and
signed off by NEDs. That I contend was a mixture of executive
capture and the mysterious way incentive risks are not assessed
in the same way as other risks.

The risks inherent in executive incentive schemes are pretty
obvious, which begs a question: how are these risks assessed and
under who's oversight are the risks mitigated? One would expect
to find risks appearing on the risk register and being reported
through to and overseen by the board risk committee. Curiously,
this is often not so for risks arising out of incentive schemes.

**Governance and Risk Management**

Commenting on the failure of the Seattle based Bank of
United States in 1933 historian Susan Kennedy[5] notes:

> *"....the closing of the Bank of United States illustrated that*
> *combination of inept management, government timidity, and*
> *impersonalisation of finance which had brought down more*
> *than 5,000 banks during the 1920s..."*

The issue of inept management manifested itself numerous
times in evidence taken by the Parliamentary Commission on
Banking Standards in 2012/13. The ineptitude ranged across
ignorance of how banks work, inattention to risks, inability to

understand the importance of the culture at the front line, let alone understand what this was and how and why this was at variance with policy set by the Board. This latter point is made in the Straumann[6] report into UBS.

> *"Some client advisors concluded that the Bank's management was not, in fact, serious about the literal application of the new US regulations"...*[7]

Governance failure was evident in bank rescues at the time of the great depression. As already noted Continental Illinois did not only fail in 1984, it had also failed in 1932. Jones and Angley write of the 1932 failure:

> *'Continental Illinois was one of the relatively few large banks in which we required a strengthening of the management....the President of the bank being heavily in debt to it".*[8]

Separated by 24 years and 4,100 miles the failures of Continental Illinois for the second time in 1984 and HBoS in 2008 are startlingly similar, as shown below.

| A Common Back Story | Continental Illinois National Bank (CINB)—Source 1 below | Halifax Bank of Scotland (HBoS)—Source 2 below |
|---|---|---|
| Aggressive growth strategies..... | In 1976, CINB's top management embarked upon an ambitious program of growth and market expansion intended to raise CINB ... to one of the three top US banks serving industry. Ch2 p4 | HBOS set a strategy for aggressive, asset-led growth across divisions over a sustained period. This involved accepting more risk across all divisions of the Group. over a sustained period. P8 |
| Resulting in major asset growth..... | 1977 -1981 16% CAGR Ch2 p4 | 2001-2008 13% CAGR p17 |
| Putting strain on funding..... | CINB became increasingly dependent on volatile and relatively more expensive funds ... during the 1976 through 1981 period, CINB ranked last among its peers in net liquidity. Ch2 p4 | HBoS had "the highest wholesale funding need of any of the UK (and was close to the other Big Four banks combined)".....in the longer term, the position was "untenable and unsustainable" p33 |
| Allied to poor risk management practices..... | CINB's top management failed to develop and maintain an internal loan quality control system of sufficient timeliness and thoroughness to balance the risks inherent in CINB's growth goals and centralised credit extension procedures'. Ch2 p6 | "The risk function in HBoS was a cardinal area of weakness in the bank. The status of the Group risk functions was low relative to the operating divisions". p22 |
| With regulatory engagement insufficient..... | ....the federal regulatory agency responsible for examining and supervising the bank rated its overall condition "good" and Its management "excellent". Twenty four months later CINB was fighting for its life. Ch1 p1 | An FSA review ... noted that HBoS's risk profile had improved and that it had made good progress in addressing the risks highlighted previously... p24 |
| And when the regulator did challenge, top management pushed back..... | CINB top management did not reflect an appropriate degree of regard for Comptroller and Federal Reserve warnings. Ch2 p5 | When HBoS was informed that its Basel II waiver would not be granted in June 2007, the HBoS Chairman wrote to the Chairman of the FSA in intemperate terms ... p27 |
| Resulting in immense failures..... | The rescue of Continental dwarfs the combined guarantees and outlays of the Federal Government in the Lockheed, Chrysler and New York City. Ch1 p2 | This percentage [of loan losses] was more than twice as high as the next largest proportion of loans incurred by a leading UK domestic commercial banking group ... p38 |
| That both inquiries found to have the same root cause. | The problems of Continental Illinois National Bank (CINB) were the direct result of decisions made at the highest management level. Ch2 p4 | The strategy set by the Board from the creation of the new Group sowed the seeds of its destruction. p8 |

Source 1: [9] Source 2: [10]

Continental had been acquiring loan portfolios from Penn Square. But, because Penn Square was underwriting very badly and because Continental's risk management system was weak, Continental wound up with large quantities of poor loans. When Penn Square failed Continental discovered that many of the loans it had bought were having their interest paid by Penn Square to disguise the fact the borrowers were in default.

This testimony from Penn Square management sets the scene for the failure:

*Well, sir, I guess the point that you are probably after, and maybe I can help you reach that point, is that the growth of the bank had been so dynamic that it had literally out-stripped its management, its people, its personnel, its physical plant. That growth had been so rapid that the personnel had not been hired to cope with it.* [11]

Testimony was then heard from Continental Illinois:

*Although our investigation of the Penn Square transactions is not completed, it has progressed sufficiently that I can tell you that we believe that our problem in Penn Square was with human error, not with the bank's procedures* [12].

This testimony, just two years before Continental was itself to fail ignored the state of Continental's underwriting and risk management processes. Despite this poor infrastructure Continental Illinois gave further reassurance to the inquiry:

*We believe that we are addressing our problems in an orderly and careful manner. We believe in our basic business principles, and we are confident that these principles, supported by the fundamental strengths of our institution and reinforced by what we have learned from this experience, provide the basis for a successful future* [13].

Three years later the inquiry into the failure of Continental Illinois heard that Federal supervisors had found significant problems in Continental's underwriting and risk management processes going back years before the Penn Square failure.

*.....the examiners on the scene did spot troubles in the internal review process in the late 1970's and early 1980's.* But, it is not apparent that OCC [The US regulator, the Office of the Comptroller of the Currency] *ever really did anything about the information—anything that might have forced the changes that might have negated the need for these hearings today.*

*In August 1981, the examiner reported the startling information that the internal review process was so badly in disarray that billions in loans had never even reached the review stage within the bank—finding $2.4 billion untouched 1 year, $1.6 billion in another year.*[14]

A further example from fifty years earlier shows the same risk management failures. The Pecora Inquiry into the numerous 1920s and 30s USA bank failures had this to say:

*The failure of the Guardian Trust Co. was not the result of unusual economic conditions, but rather the result of many years of mismanagement. Leniency in the granting of credit and laxity in collection gradually forced this bank into activities beyond the legitimate scope of banking. The bank became, in effect, a real-estate company and the holder of worthless securities.*[15]

Guardian was one of the most egregious failures in the US in the 1930s with its loan management so poor that it wound up owning worthless property through repossessions.

The first Barings failure in 1895 could also be cited as an example of poor risk management given the loans it made in South America produced such a severe loss as to threaten the bank requiring its rescue by the Bank of England.

These observations pointing to failures of leadership and risk management should not be dismissed lightly, banks are risk taking businesses.

The failure of many banks in the 2007/8 crisis appears to have been due to all three *causes* and Bagehot says this about the great failure of Overend and Gurney in 1866:

> *...and these losses were made in a manner so reckless and so foolish, that one would think a child who had lent money in the City of London would have lent better.*[16]

Jones and Angley support this view of *characteristics* and *causes* when they observe:

> *Between January 1921 and September 1930 more than ten thousand banks in the United States went out of existence - a truly shameful record for the richest country on earth. Many of these crashes were caused by bad management.*[17]

In summary then we should expand our previous thought: 'it's the capital stupid' by adding 'and poor governance'.

1. Common Factors in Bank Failures - C.A.E. Goodhart Financial Markets Group London School of Economics - written evidence to the Parliamentary Commission on Banking Standards 2012
2. Fannie Mae and Freddie Mac – Turning the American Dream into a Nightmare—Oonagh McDonald—Bloomsbury Academic—September 2013
3. The Lost Bank: The Story of Washington Mutual-The Biggest Bank Failure in American History by Kirsten Grind
4. Final Report Of The National Commission On The Causes Of The Financial And Economic Crisis In The United States Submitted By The Financial Crisis Inquiry Commission -21 January 2011
5. The Banking Crisis of 1933, Susan Easterbrook Kennedy
6. The UBS Crisis in Historical Perspective. Expert Opinion prepared for delivery to UBS AG 28 September 2010 - Dr. Tobias Straumann, University of Zurich
7. Ibid.

8. Fifty Billion Dollars – The History of the Reconstruction Finance Corporation, J H Jones and E Angley

9. U.S. Congress. House. Committee on Banking, Finance & Urban Affairs. Sub. on Financial Institutions Supervision, Regulation and Insurance. Continental Illinois National Bank: Report Of An Inquiry Into Its Federal Supervision And AssistanceContinental Illinois is interesting in itself as a failure because of the testimony given at the inquiry into a previous failure, that of Penn Square Bank.

10. House of Lords House of Commons Parliamentary Commission on Banking Standards 'An accident waiting to happen': The failure of HBOS Fourth Report of Session 2012-13

11. Penn Square Bank failure—Hearings Before The Committee On Banking, Finance And Urban Affairs House Of Representatives Ninety-Seventh Congress Second Session—Part 1 August 1982

12. Ibid.

13. Ibid.

14. Inquiry Into Continental Illinois Corp. And Continental Illinois National Bank–Hearings Before The Subcommittee On Financial Institutions Supervision, Regulation And Insurance Of The Committee On Banking, Finance And Urban Affairs House Of Representatives Ninety-Eighth Congress Second Session September 18, 19 And October 4, 1984

15. Stock Exchange Practices—Report Of The Committee On Banking And Currency page 302—16 June 1934

16. Lombard Street : a description of the money market by Walter Bagehot —1873

17. Fifty Billion Dollars – The History of the Reconstruction Finance Corporation, J H Jones and E Angley

# 10

# POLITICAL LOBBYING

I t is in management's interests to gain advantage in law and regulation to improve returns. For instance, as we have already seen, regulatory demands for banks to have more capital are met with a strong push back: "to do so will impact the real economy by reducing lending". That this argument is at best misleading and at worst dishonest does not stop it being peddled.

The separation of investment banking activity to the extent it cannot fund itself with personal savers deposits has been a long running debate, and exemplifies the effectiveness of bank lobbying over a long term.

Separation of securities trading from bank deposit taking was the subject of legislation in the US National Bank Act of 1864 which prohibited banks from trading in securities. As you will read below banks have serially abused this prohibition on an almost continuous basis such that the US Congress has made three attempts since 1864 to separate the activity: in the Federal Reserve Act of 1913, the Glass Steagall Act of 1933 and now the most recent attempt The Volcker Rule within the Dodd-Frank Act of 2010, which ran into intensive lobbying as Admati and Hellwig confirm:

> *In the United States, regulations are often watered down in*
> *response to bank lobbying. For example, in passing the Dodd-*
> *Frank Act in 2010, Congress weakened the so-called Volcker*
> *Rule, which prohibits commercial banks from trading securities*
> *on their own account. Lobbying also affects the so-called rule-*
> *making process by which the regulatory bodies implement the*
> *law*[1].

One of the main challenges the Volcker Rule has faced is defining a speculative transaction. The same transaction can for one party be speculative but for another a perfectly respectable hedge against a future risk or a straightforward commercial transaction. That this is a struggle for regulators now should not come as any great surprise as evidence given in 1931 by the Governor of the Federal Reserve shows:

> *Governor HARRISON: First of all, I do not see how any of us*
> *can define what a speculative loan is. I have tried my hardest*
> *to but I cannot define it and never have been able to find*
> *anybody who could define it in any fashion that would not work*
> *an injustice on perfectly legitimate borrowing.*[2]

The Volcker Rule is simply the latest twist in a story that has unfolded in the USA since the National Bank Act was passed in 1864. Despite this federal law prohibiting banks from trading in securities we find in a number of early twentieth century inquiries the banks had effectively circumvented the law on this point and were happily trading securities.

There were several 'panics' in US banking at the start of the 20th century with the panic of 1907 being particularly severe. As a result, the US held a number of inquiries of which three: the 1909 Governor Hughes Report,[3] National Monetary Commission 1909-1912[4] and the 1913 House of Representatives Pujo Report,[5] are informative.

Evidence from Pujo in 1913 clearly shows banks setting up security companies around 1908 specifically to avoid enforcement of the legal separation of commercial and investment banking as originally set out in the 1864 National Bank Act:

*This company was organised in February, 1908 ... under an agreement requiring that the stock of the security company shall always be owned by the same persons who own the stock of the bank and in the same proportions, and that no person not a director of the bank shall be a director of the security company.* [6]

*The purpose of the stockholders of the bank in organising the security company was to continue together in a kind of business— buying, selling, dealing in, and holding corporate stocks—which some years before the bank had been advised by the Comptroller of the Currency it could not lawfully do.* [7]

The oral evidence behind the inquiry, voices from history, illuminates this narrative in compelling fashion:

*Mr. UNTERMYER. Then the purpose of organising the security company was to do things that the bank could not lawfully do? Was that it?*

*Mr. BAKER. Yes, sir. To do things that they were not specially authorised to do. If you will let me explain right here?*

*Mr. UNTERMYER. Certainly, if you would like to do so. Proceed.*

*Mr. BAKER. The question about the legality or lawfulness of a bank's holding stock was a question that only came up for consideration in that way of later years...The purchase of bank stocks or any other stocks for years and years was never questioned by the comptroller.*

*Mr. UNTERMYER. Until when?*

*Mr. BAKER. Until probably 10 years ago.*

*Mr. UNTERMYER. And for how many years did you continue to carry stocks in the First National Bank after the right to do so was questioned?*

*Mr. BAKER. Probably for five or six years, I should think: but after we were told that we absolutely must not do it, we stopped it.*

From this we can we see the bank had avoided the 1864 law up until around 1903, and also that when challenged, it had effectively ignored the regulator for another five years. It then created a mechanism through the creation of a sister company that allowed it to continue, "to do things that they were not specially authorised to do".

The evidence gathered led to support by the majority of Pujo's committee for anti-trust laws and separation of commercial and investment banking. The committee identified the danger that deposit balances might be used to fund speculative activities:

**Pujo report. p155**

*Your committee is of opinion that national banks should not be permitted to become inseparably tied together with security holding companies in an identity of ownership and management. These holding companies have unlimited powers to buy and sell and speculate in stocks. It is unsafe for banks to be united with them in interest in management. The temptation would be great at times to use the bank's funds to finance the speculative operations of the holding company.*

*The success and usefulness of a bank that holds the people's deposits are so dependent on public confidence that it cannot be safely linked by identity of stock interest and management with a private investment corporation of unlimited powers with no public duties or responsibilities and not dependent on public confidence. The mistakes or misfortunes of the latter are too likely to react upon the former.*

Despite the majority of evidence to the contrary banks were allowed to continue with security companies, which enabled them to continue to be able to trade in securities. One can only speculate that lobbying was successful given the clarity of the Pujo findings above. The enactment of the Federal Reserve Act in 1913 which set up the central bank system in the USA did at least direct that the Federal Reserve Banks could not lend to commercial banks for speculative purposes.

This latter point was at the behest of, as he then was, Representative Glass. He would be more famous as a Senator for the 1930's Glass Steagall Act than the 1913 Federal Reserve Act which is properly known as the Owen-Glass Act. Glass was outraged by the speculative activity of the 1920s.

*He considered such activities to be a perversion of the banking system, which he helped create with the establishment of the Federal Reserve System in 1913.* [8]

### Two misconceptions Carter Glass held until 1933

Firstly, Glass had thought the Federal Reserve System he helped create in 1913 prevented banks from lending for speculative purposes. Secondly, he believed that the thousands of bank failures in the 1930s were due to speculation by banks in the 1920s bull market. He was wrong on both counts.

On the subject of banks failing due to stock market speculation, both Calomiris and Benston cast substantial doubt on whether failures caused in this way were any sort of contributory factor to the crash of 1929, and thus the Great Depression. There was however in the 1920s substantial borrowing by bank directors from their own banks in the USA, and much of this appears to have been used to speculate in one way or another in markets.

In his comprehensive analysis of the evidence from the Glass and Pecora hearings Benston[9] finds <u>no evidence</u> that speculation brought down banks. A view supported by a report into 225 bank failures by the Federal Reserve,[10] where security speculation is cited only once, amongst a number of other minority and some-what bizarre reasons for failure of banks between 1921 and 1931.

> *Other criticisms occurring only once* [out of the 225 total] *were:* **security speculation by owners***: director also director of competing bank: reinstatement of objectionable officer: excessive drinking of cashier: purchase of criticisable paper from brokers who are large shareholders: loss of memory by officer: purchase of bank by promoters.*

However, nothing is entirely clear as this testimony of a member of the Federal Reserve Board shows:

> *If we had not had these affiliated institutions in 1928 and 1929, we should not have had as bad a situation, speculatively, as we have had, I am satisfied. Some of the banks of the country have not been operated strictly and only as banks of discount and deposit. Some of them have at times had a major interest in the operations of their affiliates. To speak frankly, some of these affiliates have been little more than market operators. By reason of their access to the credit facilities of the banks with which they are affiliated, and the access of the banks to the Federal reserve system, it has been made very easy for investment affiliates to spread into dangerous zones[11].*

Whatever the arguments the view that speculative trading

caused bank failures during the 1920s and 1930s prevailed and found substance in Glass-Steagall.

On the second misconception Glass was astonished to discover in hearings he chaired in 1931 that it was impossible for Federal Reserve Banks to establish whether member banks lent for speculative, as opposed to commercial purposes. The simple reason is that a central bank in the normal course of business will from time to time lend to a commercial bank to allow overnight balancing of the books. This is however on a net basis, it was therefore impossible for the Federal Reserve to know what element if any of the net position was 'speculative'.

The exchanges between Senator Glass Chairing the inquiry in 1931 and Governor Harrison of the Federal Reserve became at times intemperate on the part of Senator Glass as he was made to confront the limitations of 'his' Federal Reserve in controlling speculation.

Glass's frustration is clear when he says at one point to Governor Harrison:

> *"You think then that this law is practically futile and a dead letter?"*

The following table summarises this long history of lobbying.

| 1864 | National Bank Act prohibits commercial banks from trading in securities |
|------|------|
| 1900 | By this time commercial banks were trading and holding securities. Around this time the Office of the Comptroller of the Currency tells banks to stop |
| 1907 | The US suffers several bank panics due to speculation, leading to a number of inquiries. |
| 1912 | A congressional inquiry reveals banks have used affiliate companies to trade in securities, the banks dispute this was to circumvent the National Bank Act |
| 1913 | Glass-Owen Act sets up the Federal Reserve System. This is thought to stop banks lending for speculative purposes |
| 1920s | Massive volumes of speculative transactions follow, this rampant stock exchange speculation ends with the crash of October 1929 |
| 1930s | Senator Glass discovers the Federal Reserve Banks were not able to stop lending for speculative purposes. Glass-Steagall is enacted |
| 1960s | ...and onwards to 1999, Glass-Steagall is progressively lobbied against and |
| 1990 | J P Morgan win authority from the Federal Reserve to trade and sell corporate stocks becoming the first commercial bank in six decades to return to the business of underwriting securities — source 3 below |
| 1999 | Gramm-Leach-Bliley Act repeals Glass-Steagall — "the long-overdue demise of a Depression-era relic" — source 4 below |
| 2000s | Massive volumes of effectively speculative transactions follow in the 2000s culminating in the banking crisis of 2008 |
| 2008 | US Congress accepts legislation to separate some investment banking from Commercial banking via The Volcker Rule |

Source 3[12] Source 4[13]

There is a circularity to these events.

**1.** It may be stretching many points to combine three periods (1907, 1920s and 2000s) of speculative frenzy. However, it is noticeable that despite the difference in the component causes of these crises they followed periods when banks were able to bring commercial and investment banking together. An important distinction between commercial banking and investment banking is the customer relationship aspect. Commercial banking, helping individuals and business finance themselves over the medium term depends on good long-term relationships. Versus, an investment banking model where part of the trading aspect is purely transactional: there is no customer to relate to when in effect the transaction in question is a one time 'bet', me against you.

**2.** Lobbying in the context of ring-fencing and/or separating banks dates back to at least 1913, although we can trace evasion back to 1903 and infer earlier than that. The 1912 Pujo inquiry wrote draft legislation, supported by the majority of the committee that recommends separating commercial and investment banking. However, for reasons I have not been able to discover, this did not make its way into the 1913 Federal Reserve Act or 1914 Anti Trust Act.

**3.** Lobbying to reduce Glass-Steagall started in the 1960s. In 1987 banks put forward the argument that regulators had improved and thus they could be allowed to combine commercial and investment banking.

*Thomas Theobald, then vice Chair of Citicorp, argues that three "outside checks" on corporate misbehaviour had emerged since 1933: **"a very effective" SEC**: knowledgeable investors, and "very sophisticated" rating agencies.*[14]

It is interesting that more or less the same argument that regulators would prevent trouble was advanced to Pujo in 1913.

*Mr. UNTERMYER. Then do I understand the only check you would suggest ... ... is the check of the Comptroller of the Currency .....?*

*Mr. SCHIFF. Well, I say in general, yes: but prudent management must have its voice in it.*

**4.**The biggest bank in the 1900s, and a major player in the 1920s (with its own securities affiliate throughout) was National City Bank, the ancestor of Citigroup which lobbied strongly in 1997/98 for the demise of Glass-Steagall.

*The New York Times reported that Citigroup CEO Sandy Weill hung in his office "a hunk of wood—at least four feet wide—*

*etched with his portrait and the words 'The Shatterer of Glass-Steagall.*[15] *"*

The concerns about the separation between commercial and investment banking have changed over time. The original fear, as expressed above, that an investment bank having access to the savings deposits of a commercial bank would lead to the investment bank speculating with these funds does appear questionable. Having said which there appear many instances of banks lending to their own directors, or the bank affiliate company lending to the directors who then engaged in market speculation.

What are now seen as the main reasons for separation are the different cultures of the two forms of banking and the need for banks to be 'resolvable' more easily.

On the culture point commercial banks are more focused on customer relationships, whereas investment banks, depending on the product, often lack not only a customer relationship but frequently via proprietary trading a customer at all.

It seems clear that over time standards at Barclays Group was heavily influenced by Barclays Capital, its investment bank. The influence growing as the investment banking management came to manage the whole group including the commercial bank. This was explained by the Salz independent review of the group:

> *Barclays' reputational vulnerability was amplified by its large investment bank, which it has successfully built over the past 15 years, and by having a high-profile investment banker as Group Chief Executive. Investment banks, with their complex products, financial trading activities and high bonuses, have been particularly blamed for the financial crisis.*[16]

Commenting further the report notes:

> *Despite some attempts to establish Group-wide values, the*

*culture that emerged tended to favour transactions over relationships, the short term over sustainability, and financial over other business purposes.*[17]

Resolvability is central bank jargon for dealing with a failed bank. If there is a hotch-potch of commercial and investment banking this is a far more difficult problem for central banks than if there is separation. Separation, even if by subsidiaries under a common holding company means that a failure of the investment bank need not mean a failure of the commercial bank, and vice versa.

The impact of the hotch-potch approach on too big to fail is without doubt. The lucky investment bank that finds itself indivisibly linked to a savings deposit funded bank knows it cannot easily be let fail for fear that losses will be inflicted upon ordinary savers. To that extent an investment bank can speculate with savers deposits.

It is clear then that the separation saga is not new, and serves as a great lesson of the power of the bank lobby, stretching back over 150 years.

---

1. The Bankers' New Clothes: What's Wrong with Banking and What to Do about It by Anat Admati, Martin Hellwig
2. Operation of the National and Federal Reserve Banking Systems Hearings Before A Subcommittee Of The Committee On Banking And Currency United States Senate Seventy-First Congress Third Session —1931
3. Report of Governor of New York, Charles E Hughes, Committee on speculation in securities and commodities, June 7, 1909
4. This commission was created by the Aldrich-Vreeland Act in 1908 in reaction to the Panic of 1907. It studied the history of central banking in the United States, as well as the central banks of Europe. The 30 reports issued by the commission informed creation of the Federal Reserve Act of 1913.

5. Report of the committee appointed pursuant to house resolutions 429 and 504 to investigate the concentration of control of money and credit 1913
6. Pujo Report p67
7. Pujo Report p68
8. The Separation of Commercial and Investment Banking - Benston - 1990
9. Ibid.
10. 225 Bank suspensions case histories from examiners' reports - Material prepared for the Federal Reserve System by the Federal Reserve Committee on Branch, Group, and Chain Banking 1932
11. Statement Of A. C. Miller, Member Of The Federal Reserve Board— Hearings Before A Subcommittee Of The Committee On Banking And Currency United States Senate Seventy-First Congress Third Session— Pursuant To S. Res. 71 A Resolution To Make A Complete Survey Of The National And Federal Reserve Banking Systems
12. NY Times—obituary of Sir Dennis Weatherstone—http://www.nytimes. com/2008/06/18/business/18weatherstone.html?_r=0
13. Frontline—The Long Demise of Glass Steagall—https://www.pbs.org/ wgbh/pages/frontline/shows/wallstreet/weill/demise.html
14. The Long Demise of Glass Steagall—PBS—Frontliner—8 May 2003 https://www.pbs.org/wgbh/pages/frontline/shows/wallstreet/ weill/demise.html
15. Final Report Of The National Commission On The Causes Of The Financial And Economic Crisis In The United States Submitted by The Financial Crisis Inquiry Commission Pursuant to Public Law 111-21 January 2011
16. Salz Review, An Independent Review of Barclays' Business Practices
17. Ibid.

# 11

# CHALLENGES TO THE REGULATOR ARISING FROM LOBBYING

The Comptroller of the Currency Mr Murray, in his 1911 report to Congress, recommended action be taken against the bad practice of directors borrowing from their own banks to finance their own interests. A year later this was picked up by the Pujo inquiry.

> *Mr. UNTERMYER. Has any action been taken on that recommendation, Mr. Murray?*
>
> *Mr. MURRAY. Nothing, except that I have received some letters of criticism for making the recommendation.*

This reaction against the regulator, letters of criticism, was not dissimilar to that described by the Governor of the Bank of England in oral evidence to the UK Parliamentary Commission on Banking Standards 102 years later.

> *Sir MERVYN KING: ......That was the climate in which the regulators operated then. It was extraordinarily difficult. They knew that if they were tough on a bank, the chief executive would go straight to No. 10 or No. 11 and say this was an*

*attack on the UK's most successful industry—even when it was*
*a perfectly reasonable application of the regulations.*

I have no knowledge of who wrote the letters of criticism to
the Comptroller in 1911, but we might infer lobbying by or on
behalf of bank directors opposed to the idea that such loans be
curtailed.

As we saw earlier, the failure of Continental Illinois for the
first time in 1932 found the bank president to be a heavy
borrower from his own bank, some twenty years after the above
evidence was given by Mr Murray. Also, one of the most egregious failures of the 1930s, The Guardian Trust Group of
Chicago, was found to have extensive loans in favour of the
directors:

*Regardless of the nature of security, to loan a sum exceeding*
*the combined surplus and undivided profits of a bank to a small*
*group* [the Directors] *of this nature violates every principle of*
*conservative banking and shows very clearly the selfish*
*manner in which depositors' funds were used by the bank*
*management.*[1]

We can tell therefore that lobbying allowed bankers to
continue to borrow from their own banks in the 1930s despite the
Comptroller's recommendation in 1911.

Regulators cannot be spared criticism, and should not be, but
it is always worth reflecting that any criticism from the industry
may well have lobbying at its heart.

### Historical conclusions

The damage banks can cause to national economies and thus
the lives of millions of ordinary citizens is plain to see in 2020,
just as it was plain to see in the 1930s. The importance of rising

to the leadership challenge of instilling and using memory to mitigate future failures is equally plain.

Whilst this may sound easy, these quotes from J K Galbraith serve as a warning that it is not. Galbraith penned these words in 1954, 25 years after the Great Depression about which he was writing.

> *"There is merit in keeping alive the memory of those days ..... It is the recollection of how, on some past occasion, illusion replaced reality and people got rimmed"...... "For protecting people from the cupidity of others and their own, history is highly utilitarian. It sustains memory and memory serves the same purpose as the SEC and, on the record, is far more effective".[2]*

Sobering words which all too sadly resonate some sixty years later with the words of Sir Christopher Kelly concerning failures at the Co-op Bank in the UK.

> *Most of the lessons are not new. Some of them are so basic that it should be a matter of considerable regret to those involved in the past management and governance of the Bank and Group that they needed to be learnt again.[3]*

Truly there is nothing new under a banking sun.

---

1. Hearings before the committee on Banking and Currency US Senate part 18—Reports on Cleveland Banking Investigation, 1934
2. The Great Crash 1929, J K Galbraith
3. Failings in management and governance—Report of the independent review into the events leading to the Co-operative Bank's capital shortfall —Sir Christopher Kelly 30 April 2014

# 12

# WHAT INSURERS ARE FOR AND HOW THEY FAIL

The repetitive nature of bank failure does raise the question are banks different? In one way they are. Banking is the only sector that can support and develop or damage national economies. But, given the root of bank failure lies in governance could other sectors have the same problems?

To get at the answer to this question I am now going to take a brief detour into the world of insurance. How do insurers work and fail and what does history tell us of the reasons for failure?

Insurance done well, like banking, provides great social benefits.

Imagine for a moment a world where no property insurance was available. The owner of the property assuming liability for fire, flood, theft and subsidence. The impact on people's willingness to invest in property would be profound.

The broad classes of insurance, general and life do not separate insurers in the same way as the broad classes of banking: retail and investment.

Insurers, general and life, have similar business models. They collect premiums, earn investment income on those premiums and pay out legitimate claims. The idea being that total premiums collected plus investment income from the premiums is greater than the amount of claims paid out. What could be simpler?

Life insurers, providing life cover, pensions and annuities may enter contracts of up to fifty years duration. Likewise, general insurers providing health or workplace insurance may take on generational liabilities.

Insurance is a promise to pay out at some future time against a justifiable claim. An inquiry into some insurance failures in the USA in the 1980s explains the nature of this promise:

> *When an insurer wrongfully fails to honour its promise to pay, the whole concept of insurance also fails. A promise is an intangible whose value is entirely dependent upon an insurer's willingness and ability to pay. Because the insurer accepts prepayment of premiums, often years in advance, there is a special responsibility to act in a manner that assures both sides of the contract will be met. The expectation that an insurance company will be around to pay legitimate claims is the first and most basic consumer right of every policyholder.* [1]

The report goes on to explain the simplicity of setting up an insurer:

> *Insurance is an easy business to enter. Because making promises does not require expensive plants and equipment or time-consuming construction, all that is really necessary is to meet regulatory capital and skill requirements, and convince potential customers that the promise of insurance will be honoured at an attractive price. The cash flow is up front, and the payment of insurance claims can be years away.* [2]

But, in a final extract from the report the complexity of operation is contrasted with the simplicity of set up:

*The simplicity of the insurance concept is matched by extreme complexity in its implementation. Pricing the promise properly, managing funds, sharing risks through reinsurance, establishing adequate reserves, and handling claims all require sound judgment, good organisation, and personal talent.* [3]

Insurance companies have two key sources of income. Premiums paid by policyholders and investment income earned on premiums collected but not yet paid out in claims. The two main expense areas are in running the insurance firm and meeting the cost of claims paid. This basic model is shown below.

From this one can tell that Insurers do not make money simply from the contents of their balance sheets as banks do. The simplified insurance balance sheet below shows this.

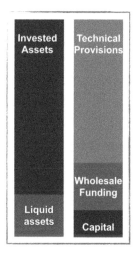

There are some similarities with banks: liquid assets, wholesale funding and capital play the same parts.

The other two blocks: invested assets and technical provisions need further explanation.

Invested assets are the premiums the insurer has received but which have not been paid out in claims. Investing these assets to provide an income is of major importance. As is trying to align the longevity of these assets with the likely longevity of promises to pay in the future. For instance, a pension not due for payment for forty years may be invested in long term assets as opposed to cash. Thus providing a better return.

Technical provisions are a financial estimate of the promises to pay claims made by the insurer to policyholders. This provisioning is a key activity for insurers. Estimating future claims correctly is crucial and complex.

The capital point is best understood if we imagine this insurer will accept no new business, it is in 'run off'. This means that the assets remain invested to pay out claims as they fall due. If over time the claims match the technical provisions, the forecast of the claims that will fall due, then the assets reduce by that amount over time. Assets are further reduced as the wholesale borrowing is paid off leaving assets to the amount of the dark blue capital block.

It is clear that the liabilities side of the balance sheet is where the big difference between banks and insurers is found. A bank funds its assets through liabilities, be this savings or wholesale debt. In contrast, the insurer has no such certain liabilities. An insurers liabilities are estimates of claims due sometime in the future. This fundamental difference shows up in the different way insurers fail.

Insurers are quite likely to suffer insolvency in the same way as banks, through poor asset selection and subsequent loss. The insurers portfolio of invested assets has, as the name says, to be invested. This investment can be done as badly as we have seen some banks lend and thus the impact on capital is the same, as shown below.

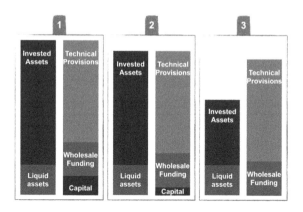

The story is like the bank example. At Point 1 the insurer is trading comfortably and well capitalised. At Point 2 losses in the asset portfolio have caused a reduction in the capital. Further losses at 3 have left the insurer insolvent. Which means policyholders future claims may not be paid out in full or at all.

A failure peculiar to insurers is that technical provisions are inadequate.

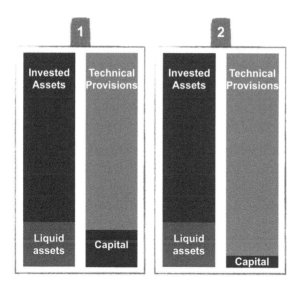

This is reflected at Point 2 above where the claims experience leads the insurer to recalculate the Technical Provisions to a much higher level. What has happened is that the insurer has underpriced the risk and collected insufficient premiums to cover the future claims. You will notice that the increase in technical provisions is matched by a reduction in capital. Again, this is best understood if you think of the insurer in run off. As the claims fall due they consume assets, because the claims are higher than originally forecast the capital left over is less.

The re-estimation of the technical provisions could have been because subsequent events have turned out very differently. This is always a big issue for insurers who take on generational risk. The increased life expectancy of pensioners for instance or the onset of critical illness claims decades after the causal workplace conditions. Equally, this could have been caused by unwise under-pricing to gain market share.

Equitable Life failed in the UK in 2000 due to a guarantee it had put in place in many of its annuities. This guarantee provided a minimum payout. During high inflation and high interest times this had not been triggered. As UK inflation fell the level of the guarantee became higher than the reducing market rates of return. It then became the preferred option exercised by policyholders as they came to take their annuities as income. Future liabilities for claims were far greater than the invested assets on hand to meet payments.

There was nothing wrong in principal with the guarantee Equitable Life had offered. Its mistake was believing it did not need to make a technical provision for this promise.

An insurance company needs to invest the premiums it receives from policy holders. Two classes of asset it will invest in are the wholesale debt and the share capital of banks, shown below.

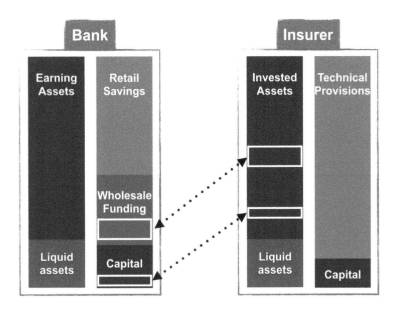

Every debit having a credit the insurer's assets are the bank's liabilities.

During the crisis of 2007/8 bank asset losses mounted. What should have happened is that the bonds and shares of banks should have been written down or even written off. But, rather than risk 'contagion', governments 'bailed-out' the banks with taxpayer funds.

The concern is if the insurance sector believes it had "a good crisis". The truth is that insurers had a better crisis because taxpayers bailed out banks. Thus insurers were not 'bailed in' taking losses on their bank shares and bonds.

---

1. Failed Promises Insurance Company Insolvencies—A Report By The Subcommittee On Oversight And Investigations Of The Committee On Energy And Commerce U.S. House Of Representatives—February 1990
2. Ibid.
3. Ibid.

# 13

# WHAT CAUSES INSURERS TO FAIL?

W e found when discussing bank failure that there were three causes: governance, risk management and incentives and we need to find out whether these three causes read across to insurance.

In 2002 an insurance working party of the European Union examined in some detail case studies put forward by EU insurance regulators. The working party described 'causal chains' comprising: *the inappropriate risk decision, the external 'trigger event' or the resulting adverse financial outcomes*[1].

The working party went on to describe how these causal chains were generated by underlying internal causes: ......*being problems with management or shareholders or other external controllers: these problems included incompetence or operating outside their area of expertise, lack of integrity or conflicting objectives, or weakness in the face of inappropriate group decisions.*[2]

The conclusion of the working party was that the causal chains, impacted by the internal causes went on to become failures in a number of similar ways: *These underlying internal problems then led to inadequate internal controls and decision-*

*making processes, resulting in inappropriate risk decisions. The firm was now vulnerable to the external 'trigger event' which caused adverse financial outcomes and, in some cases, policy-holder harm.*[3]

We have evidence here then of governance and risk management failings.

Another source of evidence of how insurers fail is found in the reports of AM Best[4] whose September 2010 report finds that:

*1. The companies, in general, were small, relatively new, and/or concentrated in one line of business or state.*

*2. Indicators of poor management were apparent, as evidenced by inadequate levels of reinsurance, rapid premium growth, data problems, underpricing, and under reserving.*

*3. Statements of Actuarial Opinion, for the most part, did not include a robust discussion of risk, nor did they identify when there was a risk of material adverse deviation (RMAD).*[5]

The report went on to discuss in more detail the issue of poor management:

*The review of financial data for many of the companies showed evidence of poor management and decision making, including little or no reinsurance, inadequate reinsurance for the amount of risk, very rapid premium growth, significant adverse development, inadequate pricing, and potentially serious data problems.*[6]

The question of incentives is not raised in these reports. However, if we consider ROE. Lifting profits can be achieved in an insurer by, for instance, aggressive resistance to what should be legitimate customer claims. It can also be achieved by: under providing for future claims, generating increased market share through under pricing premiums and as with banks, share buy backs to inflate share prices.

Whilst banks may be different to insurers in terms of how they fail, they are not different in terms of the underlying causes of failure: incentives, governance and risk management.

---

1. Prudential Supervision of Insurance Undertakings, December 2002—Conference Of The Insurance Supervisory Services Of The Member States Of The European Union
2. Ibid.
3. Ibid.
4. A.M. Best Company is a global full-service credit rating agency dedicated to serving the insurance industry. It began assigning credit ratings in 1906, making it the first of today's rating agencies to use symbols to differentiate the relative creditworthiness of companies—http://www3.ambest.com/ratings/default.asp
5. Property/Casualty Insurance Company Insolvencies September 2010—Developed by the Financial Soundness/Risk Management Committee of the American Academy of Actuaries
6. Ibid.

# 14

# WHAT ABOUT REGULATORS AND SUPERVISORS?

*The supervisory approach entailed inadequate focus on the core prudential issues of capital, liquidity and asset quality, and insufficient willingness to challenge management judgements and risk assessments[1].*

The self critical quote above is from the FSA Board report into the failure of Royal Bank of Scotland Group. The criticism the FSA board levelled at itself is not uncommon. Garth, Caprio and Levine[2] ask:

*"Can financial regulators be trusted? Out-and-out dishonesty is pretty rare. But all the evidence suggests that the regulators are buffeted by forces (psychological, bureaucratic and pecuniary) that make them unreliable protectors of the public interest".*

They go on to point out specific failings in the US, Ireland and the UK:

*Why, for example, did U.S. regulators not react to the alarming increases in leverage at financial institutions, or the shift of trillions of dollars of assets from banks' balance sheets that were packaged into complex securities?*

*Why were Irish regulators willing to sit around for two-and-a-half years waiting for a reply to a letter they sent to the Anglo Irish Bank expressing concerns about its meteoric (and unsustainable) growth?*

*Why did U.K. regulators give the Northern Rock bank a blue ribbon for risk management, and allow it to increase dividends just three months before it failed[3]?*

Regulators failing to take decisive, timely action to get a bank to change direction is not new.

- 1981 Penn Square Bank—surely someone, somewhere, would have thought to double-check an institution that had a 1,500-% growth in 7 years?[4]
- 1984 Continental Illinois—Despite having warned CINB's top management … in 1979… the Comptroller took no decisive action … prior to 1982[5]
- 2007 Northern Rock —The FSA has acknowledged that there were clear warning signals about … Northern Rock's business model…did nothing to prevent the problems that came to the fore from August 2007 onwards[6]
- 2008 Washington Mutual—For the five-year period, from 2004 to 2008, OTS repeatedly identified significant problems…WaMu promised to correct the identified deficiencies, but failed to do so[7]
- 2008 HBoS—In the three years following the merger the FSA identified some of the issues that would eventually contribute to the Group's downfall…The FSA failed to follow through on these concerns…[8]

The criticism of the regulator can be withering as in the case of Continental Illinois:

> *Strangely, this same examiner—after finding this mass of loan paper lying around unchecked—wrote the Continental board of directors this nicely perfumed note: "We found it (the internal system) to be functioning well and accurately reporting the more severely rated advances to the Board and senior management".*
>
> *What kind of timid, tip toe through the tulips signal was this supposed to convey to the board of directors[9]?*

Penn Square bank is another example. As early as 1978 regulators had found problems in the way loans were underwritten. Almost a third of loan underwriting did not meet the standards required by the bank. You'd expect some action, if not by the bank then by the regulator. That neither event happened is clear from the regulator's report a full four years later:

> *At closure, classified assets totalled to 353% of gross capital funds compared to 77% at the last general examination (12/31/80), loan losses of $49MM exceeded the gross capital structure of the bank. The examiner summarised the causative factors for the increased classified as portfolio mismanagement, over-lending, absence of controls in the energy department, poor directorate supervision, and inadequate documentation overall.[10]*

Classified loans are poorly performing and/or poorly underwritten and poorly documented loans.

The ensuing federal inquiry was scathing about the role played by the regulator. But in truth this is not a new

phenomenon and sadly it is something that we saw as a feature
of 2007/8.

*The failure of Royal Bank of Scotland in October 2008 gave
rise to what HM Treasury (HMT) has described as "the biggest
bail-out in history."*[11]

By these words the Treasury Select Committee introduce
their report into the actions of the Financial Services Authority.
The Committee placed the blame for the regulators failings on
senior management, noting from the FSA's own report into the
failure of RBS:

*The fact that the Supervision Team was largely doing what was
expected of it but was following a deficient supervisory
approach, in turn clearly implies however, that the senior
management of the FSA who determined those resources,
processes and practices must have made design decisions
which were, in retrospect, seriously mistaken.*[12]

However, the committee also noted mitigating circumstances.
These had arguably led to the *deficient supervisory approach*.
The Report gives examples of the pressure that the FSA came
under from the Government. One such example refers to a Trea-
sury press release dated 24 May 2005, at the launch of the Better
Regulation Action Plan.

In the press release, the then Chancellor says:

*"... the new model we propose is quite different. In a risk based
approach there is no inspection without justification, no form
filling without justification, and no information requirements
without justification. Not just a light touch but a limited
touch".*

Another example, in the FSA Report, refers to a speech on 14 June 2006 by the then Economic Secretary to the Treasury. In the speech he said:

> *"... we must keep the UK's regulatory system at the cutting edge—the best in the world ... at all times we will apply a principled system of risk-based regulation, without unnecessary administration burdens ... nothing should be done to put at risk a light-touch, risk-based regulatory regime".*

It seems the FSA in delivering a light touch regulatory approach was doing what had been asked of it.

It is not only bank regulators who have been knocked off course. The inquiry into Equitable Life tells of regulator resistance. Combining the role of CEO and Appointed Actuary was correctly seen as a conflict of interest. Eventually the regulator gave in and allowed the same person to occupy both roles.

As the inquiry observed, this made the CEO's position "unassailable":

> *The joint holding of these offices resulted in a lack of internal challenge of the actuarial management of the Society and a greater potential for conflict of interest......* [13]

The inquiry also observed that allowing this increased the regulator's responsibility. They now had to ensure there was objectivity and no undue conflict of interest. Unfortunately this extra responsibility was not taken on:

> *However, challenge was ineffective.* [the CEO] *was frequently aggressive in his dealings with regulators. He was dismissive of regulators views and concerns. He was obstructive of scrutiny, and often failed to answer questions put to him......*

*Unsatisfactory answers were accepted without follow-up. Lines of inquiry were abandoned or postponed in the face of resistance.*[14]

Pushing back against regulators is a red flag. NEDs must be sceptical when executives say the regulator is unreasonable, intrusive or over zealous. It could well be a warning sign that the executive is in a bad situation and that the regulator is right.

1. The failure of the Royal Bank of Scotland
   Financial Services Authority Board Report—December 2011
2. Guardians of Finance Making Regulators Work for Us - Garth, Caprio and levine
3. Ibid.
4. Penn Square Bank Failure—Before The Committee On Banking, Finance And Urban Affairs House Of Epresentatives Ninety-Seventh Congress Second Session Part 1 July 15; And August 16, 1982
5. U.S. Congress. House. Committee on Banking, Finance & Urban Affairs. Sub. on Financial Institutions Supervision, Regulation and Insurance. Continental Illinois National Bank: Report Of An Inquiry Into Its Federal Supervision And Assistance
6. House of Commons Treasury Committee The run on the Rock Fifth Report of Session 2007–08
7. Wall Street And The Financial Crisis: Anatomy Of A Financial Collapse Majority And Minority Staff Report Permanent Subcommittee On Investigations United States Senate
8. House of Lords House of Commons Parliamentary Commission on Banking Standards 'An accident waiting to happen': The failure of HBOS Fourth Report of Session 2012-13
9. Inquiry into Continental Illinois Corp. and Continental Illinois National Bank - Hearings before the Subcommittee on Financial Institutions Supervision, Regulation and Insurance of The Committee on Banking, Finance and Urban Affairs, House of Representatives - Ninety-Eighth Congress Second Session September 18, 19 And October 4, 1984
10. Office of the Comptroller of the Currency - Specialised Examination March 31, 1982 Examiner in Chief, Stephen D. Plunk

11. House of Commons Treasury Committee—The FSA's report into the failure of RBS—Fifth Report of Session 2012–13—October 2012
12. Ibid.
13. Report of the Equitable Life Inquiry—The Right Honourable Lord Penrose—March 2004
14. Ibid.

# 15

# WHAT CAUSES REGULATORS AND SUPERVISORS TO FAIL?

As we see a typical failure of regulators is not an inability to spot an issue but rather, having spotted it, not acting decisively. This was a point the members of the 1982 inquiry into the Penn Square failure made clear to the federal regulators:

> *The fact of the matter is I know of nobody who will criticise you for acting too soon. I think the previous speaker is exactly right. The warning system worked: you simply didn't act.....I don't think you would be criticised if you rang the bell earlier, rather than too late. Keep that in mind.*[1]

That of course falls into the category of 'easy for you to say'.

The difficulty of a regulator taking decisive action against a bank in what appears to be a time of plenty should not be underestimated. Earlier in this book we didn't note the power of bank lobbying and the supporting shroud of jargon for nothing. Any regulator who intervenes early, when a bank appears to be doing well, is more likely to be criticised for being bureaucratic, anticompetitive and box ticking than to be congratulated for good judgement.

Understanding why supervisors might fail to intervene earlier means understanding how the supervision cycle unfolds. There are three essential stages in what is a continuous cycle shown here.

| Essential Stages of the Supervision Cycle | Commentary | Why supervisors have typically failed |
|---|---|---|
| **Judgement 1**<br><br>What do supervisors think of the firm | Supervisors will want to look at how the firm makes money, its strategy and governance, its attitude to risk and the effectiveness of risk management, balance sheet strength (capital and liquidity). Supervisors should be taking a forward looking view of the key risks the bank might pose to financial stability. | Poor analysis due to constraints of resourcing and /or experience.<br><br>Poor communication of key risks within the supervision hierarchy.<br><br>Poor senior supervisory support leading to firms able to lobby against the analysis. |
| **Judgement 2**<br><br>What action is required of supervisors/the firm | What actions does supervision expect the bank to take to strengthen itself or otherwise remediate aspects of supervision's opinion in Judgement 1 above, particularly to mitigate key risks. | Poor communication of what is required to the firm's board. |
| **Execution**<br><br>Following through on Judgement 2 | Having identified through Judgement 2 and communicated to the firm actions that are required, ensuring robust follow up and conclusion of the actions. | Indecisive action to ensure the firm deals in a timely fashion with shortcomings/risks supervisors have identified as needing remediation and mitigation.<br><br>Poor senior level support to supervisors such that firms can avoid the action required. |

A finding that late intervention tends to be the main regulatory failure is not unique to bank regulators. This is clear from the inquiry into the failure of the Mid Staffs hospital in the UK which noted a long list of warning signs:

> *Loss of star rating ...... the Commission for Health Improvement (CHI) re-rated the Trust, and it went from a three star trust to zero stars ......*
>
> *Peer reviews ...... Each of these reviews identified a number of concerns, often serious concerns, with the Trust's ability to deliver a safe service, and raised questions about management capability.[2]*

A further regulatory issue is when more than one agency is involved as this comment from the public inquiry into the Bristol Royal Infirmary makes clear:

> *What was lacking was any real system whereby any*

*organisation took responsibility for what a lay person would describe as 'keeping an eye on things'. The Supra Regional Services Advisory Group (SRSAG) thought that the health authorities or the Royal College of Surgeons was doing it: the Royal College of Surgeons thought the SRSAG or the Trust was doing it, and so it went on. No one was doing it.*[3]

Another issue that regulators struggle with is one that NEDs also struggle with, information asymmetry. The executive of the organisation will usually know more than the NEDs and the regulators. Whatever reporting is in place a dominant and/or devious management can push back forcefully against investigative or corrective action NEDs or regulators may want to see happen.

Our earlier discussion of bank failure included Galbraith's quotes. Let us remember that he wrote those in 1954 in the winter of his life in an attempt to remind people of what happened thirty years earlier in the "Roaring 20's" that caused the Great Depression of the 1930's.

It seems that as with the failure of banks and insurers we find with the failure of regulators, remembering what has gone wrong in previous crises is all too easily forgotten in times of plenty.

1. Penn Square Bank failure—Hearings Before The Committee On Banking, Finance And Urban Affairs House Of Representatives Ninety-Seventh Congress Second Session
    Part 1 July 15: And August 16, 1982
2. Report of the Mid Staffordshire NHS Foundation Trust Public Inquiry—February 2013—Robert Francis QC
3. Public Inquiry into the Bristol Royal Infirmary—2001

# 16

## SUMMARISING THE FIRST PART

This brings The First Part to a close. We have discovered that banks and insurers fail for the same reasons they always have. That regulators continue to struggle with decisive and timely action. And, that one stand out success of banking is the effectiveness of its political lobby.

We have found that weak governance ruins decision making leading to corporate failure. As statements of the obvious go this appears to be blinding. But facts culled from three centuries of public inquiries across sectors underpin it.

The Second Part takes us into new territory, what can we do? What can we do about corporate governance? And, is this applicable across industries? What about culture, is this controllable or is it an intangible boards have to live with? Is board effectiveness an elusive myth? If it isn't what are the tangible actions whereby boards can improve their effectiveness?

Finally, to what extent can we learn from the past and embed some memory into what we do today?

∼

# THE SECOND PART—WHAT CAN BE DONE

# INTRODUCTION

This Second Part is devoted to the cause of the NED and Trustee and to the effectiveness of boards. Our introduction is by the Chair of the Federal Reserve Bank of New York at an inquiry in 1931:

> *The responsibility for the solvency of banks and the safety of depositors' money must inevitably be that of bank management. Responsibility and management cannot be separated.*[1]

Do we need to re-learn that 'responsibility and management cannot be separated'? Well, in many cases of corporate failure that separation existed and so the answer is yes.

I have already said that the key to board effectiveness is honing the ability of the board to arrive at good decisions. Implicit in this is both a supporting and a challenging role for NEDs. It is interesting to reflect, if NEDs are fulfilling this dual role, is it possible to separate responsibility and management? There is undoubtedly a link because time and again in failed organisations challenge was not welcome and support had become cheer leading of the worst sort. This extract from the inquiry into the failure of HIH Insurance in Australia illustrates this:

> *There was blind faith in a leadership that was ill-equipped for the task. There was insufficient ability and independence of mind in and associated with the organisation to see what had to be done and what had to be stopped or avoided*[2].

A good NED knows how to challenge well and in my view this challenge is founded on three personal qualities: the will to challenge, the skill to challenge and the knowledge needed to challenge. The will, the skill and the knowledge is something we will return to.

A failure of NED challenge does not lead to catastrophe tomorrow, or even next year. However, over time the quality of board judgements will deteriorate, increasing the risk of disaster.

Most directors and trustees are clear that their responsibilities as members of the board are shared. For instance, responsibility for strategy is of all members of the board. However, the danger of everyone being responsible is that no-one is.

All directors, and all trustees, are not the same. There are roles such as Chair of the Board and CEO with entirely different responsibilities, not to mention Chair of Audit Committee as compared to a NED without any responsibility beyond being a NED. However, most of all there are two groups, the executives and the non-executives. The Chair of the board's role is to lead a team comprising these two groups who, when they interact positively, will optimise decision making and performance throughout the business.

Denying the existence of these two groups leads to amnesia regarding their purpose. The executives, skilled and knowledgable in their business, lead it on a full time day to day basis. The non-executives, part time and perhaps not as expert, are there to help the executives step back from the coalface, to oversee their performance and check the overall direction is right. This non-executive role involves support and mentoring as well as challenge. In a few cases it will go beyond challenge and involve control: 'no CEO, you are not going to do that' or, 'however much you don't like it you do have to do this'. In some cases it will involve the NEDs replacing the CEO.

With shared responsibility there is ample potential for the non-assumption of personal responsibility. Too many inquiries into failed organisations cite directors behaving like T S Eliot's famous cat:

> *'At whatever time the deed took place—Macavity wasn't there'.*[3]

The directors' epitaph in too many failures has been: 'No, no, no, it wasn't me: no, no, no, I wasn't there, and: no, no, no, I didn't know'.

All is not lost however, because in seeing what bad looks like we can divine what good looks like. My hope is that you will agree the NED role does have life in it, as long as we get the basics right and spend more than twenty days a year doing it.

In writing the Second Part my aim is for readers to be able to pick and choose. There is a flow but don't hesitate to interrupt the flow and head off to the bits you are most interested in.

If you do go with the flow we will start with the business model, what it is and what do NEDs need to watch for?

Why business models? Well, whatever the organisation: private, public or charitable, NEDs must understand the purpose of their organisation. They must also be sure that purpose has not been subverted by a full on charge to control costs or maximise income. NEDs must go beyond asking how much money the organisation makes and the effectiveness of its cost controls, indeed they must shun the perceived wisdom that their role is just to maximise financial value. Instead, they must be sure <u>how</u>

money is earned and what impact cost control is having on outcomes.

The next section is risk management. It is an immense subject and I've aimed to answer one question: what is it NEDs need to oversee? You'll pick up on Swiss Cheese, Cyber and one of the best risk questions there is.

We will then turn to culture. What it is and what it isn't, and you will discover that NEDs can indeed influence culture. There won't be much about ethics, values and morals, which I hope you will find as much of a joy as I do. Instead, I will explain what NEDs can do at five past nine on that rainy Monday morning.

Our finish point is the toolkit of corporate governance. When corporate governance is done right it influences purpose, the business model, risk management and the culture of the organisation.

Corporate governance is the means by which board decision making is honed and thus effectiveness is earned. The clue though is that it has little to do with terms of reference and codes and everything to do with the Chair's leadership and the consequent behaviour of the members of the board.

One of the biggest elephant traps is to imagine the board as a person or object, that getting an effective board is about the effectiveness of something known as 'the board'. The truth is, it is people working together effectively that makes boards effective. That is why this Second Part focuses on the role of the Chair and the NEDs. If they are effective, and work together effectively, then as surely as night follows day the Executives will also be effective.

As with the First Part this introduction closes with a quote from Walter Bagehot and, without apology, I repeat the words this book opens with:

*There is in all ordinary joint stock companies a fixed executive specially skilled, and a somewhat varying council not specially skilled. The fixed manager ensures continuity and experience in the management, and a good board of directors ensures general wisdom.*[4]

Ensuring general wisdom, what cracking shorthand for the role of the NED.

1. Statement Of J. H. Case, Chair Of The Board Of Directors Of The Federal Reserve Bank Of New York—Hearings Before A Subcommittee Of The Committee On Banking And Currency United States Senate Seventy-First Congress Third Session—January 1931
2. HIH Royal Commission. The failure of HIH Insurance—ISBN 0 9750678 5 0 (set)—April 2003
3. Macavity, the Mystery Cat by T S Eliot
4. Lombard Street : a description of the money market by Walter Bagehot —1873

# 17

# THE BACK STORY

L et us start the Second Part with the back story to corporate failure.

Starting with banks, as we have seen, the story goes something like this:

- An aggressive, executive led strategy leads a bank to major asset growth which leads to strain on funding those assets
- This charge to greatness by the executives is accompanied by poor non-executive oversight and regulators who are slow to keep up, often because the executives pushed back
- In the end there is an immense failure that was to all intents and purposes designed by the board

In the Great Financial Crisis in the UK we can find aspects of this at RBS, Northern Rock and HBoS. And, we found the same in previous bank failures going back to the 19th century at least.

However, it's not just banks. Aspects of this were found at Equitable Life, a large and reputable UK life insurer which closed for new business in December 2000. Its failure was so bad that policyholders lost benefits they expected to receive in retirement.

The inquiry into the failure of Equitable by Lord Penrose identified the strength of character of the Chief Executive. Whilst there was some disagreement by the Chief Executive with Lord Penrose's assessment of him the final report commented as follows:

> It may also be claimed, in mitigation of the non-executives, that the Board was dominated by [the CEO]......I note his own assessment of his approach in discussion with regulators, as 'autocratic'. That coincides with other information available to me.[1]

This dominance was exacerbated by the inability of the NEDs to challenge the CEO's powerful position, the regulator having allowed him to be both CEO and Chief Actuary.

> None of the non-executive members of the Board had relevant skills or experience of actuarial principles or methodologies over most of the reference period. They were generally experienced in the financial services industry, but specialists, where they had specialist knowledge, in general finance, in investment and banking rather than life assurance.[2]

This is a prime example of the fatal impact a lack of informed non-executive challenge has on a firm. The powerful chief executive could not be kept in check, the business fundamentals were not understood well enough by the non-executives and the tragedy that followed was in the end entirely predictable.

However, our story is not just about financial services and so we turn to the UK National Health Service. The failure at Mid Staffs NHS Foundation Trust was tragic:

*Above all, it failed to tackle an insidious negative culture involving a tolerance of poor standards and a disengagement from managerial and leadership responsibilities. This failure was in part the consequence of allowing a focus on reaching national access targets, achieving financial balance and seeking foundation trust status to be at the cost of delivering acceptable standards of care.*[3]

That there were problems with the organisation's culture is clear and this was highlighted elsewhere in the report following a review of the Accident & Emergency department:

*The treatment by management of nurses in particular was beyond belief. The nurses were threatened on a near daily basis with losing their jobs if they did not get patients out within the four hours target ... it was quite normal for nurses to come out at the end of ...* [bed management] *meetings crying*[4]

These failures had to have a root cause. From the concern shown by the inquiry into the leadership of the board and the performance of the NEDs it is clear the problem came from the top. The inquiry gives a telling description of the board:

*The Trust Board leadership between 2006 and 2009 was characterised by lack of experience, great self-confidence, a focus on financial issues, obtaining foundation trust (FT) status and meeting targets, and a lack of insight into the impact of their decisions on patient care. The non-executive leadership remained aloof from serious operational concerns even when they had obvious strategic significance and the potential for causing risk to patients.*[5]

On this latter point, non-executive aloofness was found to extend to mortality alerts, a hugely important metric for any healthcare organisation, particularly if it is an outlier for the wrong reasons:

> *In relation to mortality alerts,* [the Chair] *thought these were a matter for the Medical Director, not the Board. She did not consider the Board's role to include getting involved in what she considered to be operational detail.*[6]

Balancing all this is comment from the Chair of the Inquiry:

> *The fact that a critical comment is made about some action of an individual or an organisation does not necessarily mean that there are not many positive aspects to their work and contribution to healthcare. Many of those about whom some critical comment has been made have been involved in making significant changes for the better. Many have offered notable insights to the inquiry ...*[7]

Finally, let us take a look at the charitable sector. The House of Commons inquiry into one charity failure said this:

> *Founded in 1996 ... Keeping Kids Company (commonly known as "Kids Company") was a registered charity which stated that its aim was to provide practical, emotional and educational support to vulnerable children and young people.*[8]

The role of NEDs in a charity is assumed by the Trustees, about whom the inquiry presents us with an eerily familiar description:

> *With a complete lack of experience of youth services amongst Trustees, it was impossible for the Board to assess the appropriateness of significant expenditure that* [the CEO] *justified on the basis of clinical judgements. It is nevertheless*

*extraordinary that Trustees were content to accept this without more rigorous examination.*[9]

This problem of inexperienced trustees was exacerbated, yet again, by a powerful CEO:

*... The CEO has been described as an 'emblematic figure' who possessed extraordinary fundraising capabilities. Former employees praised the CEO for being the 'heart of our team', leading the charity 'superbly' and working 'a 6 day week minimum, typically working 10 plus hours a day'.*[10]

*The Charity Commission's guidance to Trustees warns that Trustees should not allow their judgement to be swayed by personal prejudices or dominant personalities, but this is what occurred in Kids Company. This resulted in Trustees suspending their usual critical faculties ...*[11]

Charities, banks, insurers and hospitals. Let us acknowledge that the similarities of challenges to board effectiveness, corporate governance and corporate culture are universal. They cross sectors and thus what we are about to look at has wide application, well beyond just banks.

Off we go then, I hope you enjoy the journey as much as I have enjoyed researching and writing it up.

1. Report of the Equitable Life Inquiry—The Right Honourable Lord Penrose—March 2004
2. Ibid.
3. The Mid Staffordshire NHS Foundation Trust Public Inquiry—Chaired by Robert Francis QC—Vol 1 page 9—February 2013
4. Ibid.

5. Ibid
6. Ibid.
7. Ibid.
8. House of Commons Public Administration and Constitutional Affairs Committee—The collapse of Kids Company: lessons for charity trustees, professional firms, the Charity Commission, and Whitehall—Fourth Report of Session 2015–16
9. Ibid.
10. Ibid.
11. Ibid.

# 18

# BUSINESS MODELS

I challenge you to find a Non-Executive Director[1] (NED) or Trustee who will not sign up to what Higgs wrote in 2003:

*Non-executive directors should constructively challenge and contribute to the development of strategy[2].*

However, some NEDs might hesitate over what else Higgs said:

*They [NEDs] must be well-informed about the business, the environment in which it operates and the issues it faces. This requires a knowledge of the markets in which the company operates as well as a full understanding of the company itself.[3]*

What Higgs described in 2003 is today called the business model. Understanding the purpose of the firm (and by firm I include all organisations: public, private and charitable) and why it exists is at the heart of the board's role. The business model is taking that purpose and asking the question: how does, and will, this firm make money?

Business models have three dimensions, two financial and one conduct. Conduct is about <u>how</u> business is done and therefore rests heavily on culture. The three dimensions are:

| | | |
|---|---|---|
| (1) | Viability | Is the cost of capital covered in the near term? |
| (2) | Sustainability | Is it expected the cost of capital will be covered in the medium term? |
| (3) | Conduct | Are we harming customers or the markets we operate in? |

Taking the financial dimension first, viability: is the firm able to cover its cost of capital today? Not being able to do so might be acceptable in the short term, business has cycles after all.

The second dimension asks whether the firm is sustainable? In other words is it forecast to cover its cost of capital in the medium term (let us say its planning horizon of three to five years). If the answer is no then matters are existential and we had better hope for a lot of capital, and patient and supportive owners.

In a charity or public body such as a hospital the first two dimensions simply become: are <u>costs</u> being covered in the near/medium term.

The third dimension concerns the ability of the firm to cause harm through its behaviour, which is of course rooted in its culture. Is the firm behaving in a way that causes harm to any or all of consumers, counter-parties or the markets within which it operates?

Business models have for so long been thought to rest on the financial results, viability and sustainability, that the behavioural aspect of 'how' the firm is conducting itself has often been lost. You may recall that in The First Part I referred to Barings. The board was told great profit was being made, unfortunately no-one thought to ask how. This reinforces that boards need to look as closely at star performers as units which are struggling. As one FTSE Chair put it to me during my research:

> *We make a mistake when we only interrogate the numbers in brackets. There is great danger when the board says: "thank God for Harry, he always delivers".*

The question is not just can Harry continue to deliver, but how is it he always delivers?

One way of understanding the relationship between these dimensions is to map them onto a four box model as shown here:

Profit
The viable/sustainable aspects
Loss

Bad          Good

The harm aspect (culture and behaviour)

I have simplified the first and second dimensions, viability and sustainability, to profit and loss. The third dimension, the harm that can be caused, is shown to arise from good or bad culture and behaviour. You can use the four boxes in two ways: put the whole of your business in one of the boxes or, thinking of the component parts of your business: the regions, the products, the executives, disciplines and subsidiaries split your organisation across more than one box.

Before you continue reading I'd like you to ponder how you might describe each box, keep it brief.

My thoughts on the content of the four box model are shown below and, to repeat, this can be a picture of the whole firm or broken down into parts of the firm.

Starting in the bottom right box: losing money but without causing harm is clearly a commercial problem requiring a decision.

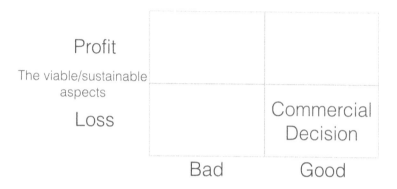

There are, or should be, one of three solutions: fix matters so that profit is made (or for a non-profit, costs covered), accept that this cannot be done and exit or, agree this is a valid cross subsidy of another part of the business. Two other options exist: not spotting the problem, or spotting it and prevaricating. I will leave both out as these are symptoms of a wider malaise.

In the top right box all is well. Profit is being made and no harm is being caused to consumers, counter-parties or markets. Although, I will caution you to remember Harry, how is it he always delivers?

| Profit<br>The viable/sustainable<br>aspects<br>Loss | | Sunlit<br>Uplands |
|---|---|---|
| | | Commercial<br>Decision |
| | Bad | Good |

The harm aspect (culture and behaviour)

This leaves us with two rather more difficult boxes. The top left I dub 'looming problem', if the firm is making money by harming one or all of consumers, counter-parties or markets then it will be found out.

| Profit<br>The viable/sustainable<br>aspects<br>Loss | Looming<br>Problem | Sunlit<br>Uplands |
|---|---|---|
| | | Commercial<br>Decision |
| | Bad | Good |

The harm aspect (culture and behaviour)

Discovery will come via an investigative journalist, an investigative regulator or a whistle blower, but it will happen. Sometimes this has taken decades, the case of Bernie Madoff took some forty years to come to light but come to light it did.

This leaves only one box, the bottom left. When I asked you to ponder four empty boxes I forgive you for thinking of this box: 'who could be stupid enough to rip someone off and still lose money?' Of course this box is not about that, this box is where you go after your harmful activities have been exposed.

The harm aspect (culture and behaviour)

Overall this is not a static model because you don't just sit in a box and stay there. Have a look at the revised four boxes below:

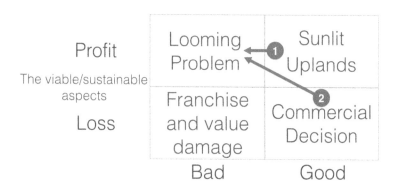

The harm aspect (culture and behaviour)

Arrow 1 describes a firm, or product/region/legal entity of

that firm, that had been making money in the right way but perhaps it was decided more money had to be made, inflicting harm somewhere. Possibly the extra profit was to come from more income. Or maybe, in a misguided attempt to improve profit by cutting costs, some control feature was lost. Either way the journey was made.

Arrow 2 describes an under performance that was fixed in the wrong way by impacting harm on someone or on markets. It perhaps describes a firm discovering the business model could not be fixed (ethically) and, not wishing to exit, the decision was taken to fix it by causing harm.

In both cases I have used the words 'decided' and 'decision' as though the board or senior management of the firm consciously undertook to pursue a harmful approach. I suspect no executive or NED is easily going to admit to such a decision. However, if the executive and/or NEDs did not know the activity had happened, and were not able to catch on before the outside world found out, then I'm afraid they failed two of Higgs' tests *...they must be well informed about the business...as well as a full understanding of the company itself.*[4]

I don't doubt the difficulty of spotting where an organisation may be causing harm especially for NEDs who are part time. The words of the NED in the introduction to The First Part ring in our ears. However, just because it is difficult does not mean it cannot be done and I hope as you read on you will see how.

I would next ask you to think about which of the four box axes (horizontal rows or vertical columns) is subject to the most rigorous management information and reporting.

The answer is the horizontal rows. Boards are served to the point of inundation by financial information that flows in from the left of the four boxes.

The vertical columns are a different matter. What information does a board get that enables it to discern whether individuals, products, regions or legal entities are in the left or right hand boxes?

Ironically, the only box where there is absolute certainty is the bottom left box. You do know if your firm, or part of it, is subject to fines, a redress scheme or some kind of deferred prosecution agreement for causing harm.

In open forum not many NEDs will plot anything in the top left box, in closed forum they might. However, it is more likely the NEDs lack enough information to say that there is dubious activity going on and therefore plotting into either of the right hand boxes is an exercise of hope over fact.

There is enough evidence in the Final Notices issued by conduct of business regulators that boards have not been assuring themselves about where their businesses are regarding the left and right hand columns. Understand the 'how' is a problem that boards have to face and solve and NEDs have a key role to play. In assuring themselves about their firm's business model they must look to both dimensions, not one, and by so doing meet Higgs imperative to be 'well informed'.

Before we go on to see how this might be done I'd like you to think in which box hubris is most likely to make an unwelcome appearance and cause harmful movement.

*Hubris often indicates a loss of contact with reality and an overestimation of one's own competence, accomplishments or capabilities.*[5]

I hope you landed in the top right hand box. This is where it is easiest for a CEO to believe his or her own ability is beyond compare and here is the place where NEDs might, on seeing the CEO's numbers, agree. The problem is that after you have started to believe in your own God-like qualities what tends to follow is unpleasant, probably involving a shift into one of the left hand boxes.

A start point for all NEDs is to think more broadly than the bottom line. For instance, being properly sceptical about success, because it has repeatedly been found that the highly profitable (firm, trader, region, product) had been in the top left box all along. Not anywhere near every time, but repeatedly enough to stand warning.

It is not confrontational to create, as part of the annual rhythm of the board, a review of all top performing areas. I remember a salesforce where the top ten salespeople were subject to more compliance checks than the majority for this very reason.

Regarding costs, a NED might ask: 'what impact will these cost savings have on our future profits?' This appears to meet the classification of challenge: tick box marked 'reasonable steps' in the compliance manual. However, the more effective challenge is to ask for evidence of the impact this will have on how we do business. Ask: 'by doing this are we more or less likely to cause harm?' The chances that cost savings, wherever they fall, result in less management or independent oversight and the risk of losing critical controls is greater than you think.

An anonymised quote from the Financial Stability Board's paper on mitigating misconduct risk provides an apt lead into considering where business models go wrong:

*Leadership's attention was focused on maximising short-term profits, and it adopted the view that success could not be achieved without compromising ethics.*[6]

---

1. Wherever I talk about NEDs take this to include Trustees too.
2. The Higgs Report, 2003 - http://www.ecgi.org/codes/documents/higgsreport.pdf

3. The Higgs Report, 2003 - http://www.ecgi.org/codes/documents/higgsreport.pdf|Ibid.
4. Ibid.
5. https://en.wikipedia.org/wiki/Hubris
6. Financial Stability Board—Strengthening Governance Frameworks to Mitigate Misconduct Risk: A Toolkit for Firms and Supervisors—20 April 2018

# 19

# WHERE BUSINESS MODELS GO WRONG

S hareholder value has been a pre-eminent measure of corporate success for decades, a focus the Financial Times bring out in their lexicon's definition of business models:

> *... ... a business model's success is reflected in its ability to create returns that are greater than the (opportunity) cost of capital, invested by its shareholders and bondholders*[1].

This is why the four box model is so important in broadening the view of business models. It forces boards to consider <u>how</u> money is being made, not just that it is being made.

The FT provide an example of a financially precarious business model, that of GM in the run up to the crisis.

> *General Motors, for many years, had an unsustainable business model as its returns did not match or exceed its cost of capital. Profitability was focused on the financing of cars, i.e., providing financing to its automotive customers, such as loans to buy the cars, through its finance subsidiary GMAC, rather than by designing and manufacturing sought after cars that are*

*also cost competitive. When the financial crisis struck, this model encountered problems, and as GMAC had to seek a US government bailout, the company's already precarious condition turned into bankruptcy[2].*

It appears that General Motors had completely lost sight of its business model and where the money it earned was supposed to come from: the development, manufacture and sale of cars.

The four box model pushes thinking to take account of how money is made, in the case of GM this should have highlighted the core business was unprofitable and depended entirely on the financial arm for adequate profits.

More extreme is the 'are we ripping anybody off' question. Now, you might not particularly enjoy the language of 'ripping off' or the concept that mature adults in responsible positions sit around agreeing to this. In which case let me illuminate the problem by asking you to consider a couple of examples, and you are a NED:

- You notice that small sub-contractors supplying your company are paid on 120 day terms, but even then the payments your company makes are often late. The CEO and FD explain this is 'intelligently maximising the company's leverage so as to positively impact the cashflow'
- You discover a large number of customers complaining that what they see as legitimate claims are being refused. These complaints are being turned away on the grounds that the claims policy is clear in the terms and conditions which have been signed off by the company lawyers

It is easy to justify 'ripping people off' as smart business practice or legally justified. The worry is of course that as well as being a rip off these tactics are desperately needed to shore up the business, just like GM and its finance arm. The worry should be that these are the tip of a rather nasty iceberg.

In developing strategy boards are looking to change the business model for the better. Strategy will be covered later but suffice to say it must not only include where we want to get to but also how we are going to get there and why.

As an example, NEDs should look askance at plans to grow market share if there is no clearly defined method for achieving this. In the UK the size of the savings market is something over one trillion sterling. It is a zero sum game and for you to attract extra market share someone has to lose it. Any strategic plan that sees a bank with, let us say 4% of the savings market, aiming to collect over any time period 8% of savings must have a serious question mark over it. What is the attraction that will convince the saver to end a current relationship and move to you? Is it price or is there some key product feature in the bank's savings lineup that others do not have?

If a market participant does take an outlier position with a product then eventually, as in any competitive market, what is known as 'regression to the mean' will take place. If the outlier position is on price then either high savings rates will have to be reduced as the bank finds it cannot stomach the downward pressure on its core margin, or others in the market will come to match the pricing, removing the outliers competitive position.

The Nobel prize winning psychologist Daniel Kahneman refers to regression in this way:

> ... ... *the statistician David Freedman used to say that if the topic of regression comes up in a criminal or civil trial, the side that must explain regression to the jury will lose the case. Why is it so hard? The main reason for the difficulty ... ... our mind is strongly biased toward causal explanations and does not deal well with "mere statistics*[3].

In other words we can't easily cope with the idea that market performance might be to do with the market itself and not the entrepreneurial genius of individuals.

Which is not to say the entrepreneurial genius of individuals does not exist as you can tell from what Steve Ballmer CEO of Microsoft had to say when Apple launched the iPhone:

*Right now, we're selling millions and millions and millions of phones a year. Apple is selling zero phones a year.*[4]

A very few years later he was telling analysts:

*"Mobile devices. We have almost no share,"*

Innovative products and services are capable of setting an organisation apart from its competitors and at the same time completely redefining a market. The trick for NEDs is to investigate diligently not only why a firm's executive are so positive about their forecast results but <u>how</u> they expect to deliver these.

A very dubious answer to 'why are we doing so well' or 'why are we <u>going</u> to do so well' is: 'through outstanding talent management we possess highly talented managers', or words to that effect. It might sound wonderful to the board to hear that the organisation has such talented people who make the organisation so attractive to customers that market share will increase, but it is as well to be sceptical about such claims in the absence of a robust business case.

And, for savings and mobile phone markets read markets for: cars, air conditioning, consultancy services, package holidays, legal services, medical services, food, cosmetics, pharmaceuticals and conjurors' props. You can also read the ability of a hospital to cut costs without cutting care standards. How? Talented managers. With fewer nurses? Talented managers.

Northern Rock Bank is another example of a business model

that was unfit for purpose. The UK Treasury Committee's report into the bank's failure noted how matters came to a head in September 2007:

> *At 8.30 pm on the evening of Thursday 13 September 2007 the BBC reported that Northern Rock plc had asked for and received emergency financial support from the Bank of England.*[5]

Eleven weeks earlier Adam Applegarth, the Chief Executive of Northern Rock had been interviewed by "Thisismoney":

> *'There are always good days and bad days,' he* [Applegarth] *smiles. The bitterness of the profit downgrade was sweetened by Northern Rock finally receiving its Basle II waiver yesterday, which will release spare capital and pave the way for 'a huge increase in dividends and share buybacks'. 'We've been waiting three years for this waiver and it comes on the same day as a profit warning,' he says wryly. 'The strange thing is, I know the share price has had a good shoeing but I also know the stuff we are announcing today will leave the company in a much better place than it is now in three years' time.'*[6]

Now you can if you wish argue that it is part of the Chief Executive's role as chief salesman for the organisation to put a positive spin on results. However, there is no sign here of any retrenchment even though financial markets were decidedly jumpy in the summer of 2007 and Northern Rock had issued a profit warning. The intended use of freed capital to fund a '*huge increase in dividends and buybacks*' suggests quite the reverse. In fact it was quite the reverse as the Treasury Committee went on to note:

> *Due to this approval* [of the Basle II waiver]*, Northern Rock*

*felt able to announce on 25 July 2007 an increase in its interim*
*dividend of 30.3%.*[7]

This interim dividend increase was announced seven weeks
before Applegarth was forced to turn to the Bank of England for
emergency liquidity assistance. A day later queues of deeply
worried customers formed outside his branches.

The fatal flaw in Northern Rock's business model was
described by the Treasury Committee on page 1 of its report into
the failure:

> *The directors of Northern Rock were the principal authors of*
> *the difficulties that the company has faced since August 2007.*
> *The directors pursued a reckless business model which was*
> *excessively reliant on wholesale funding.*[8]

The wholesale funding reliance was in part a consequence of
a risk model that said the losses on the mortgages Northern Rock
advanced would be very low. Thus we can see the intertwined
nature of strategy, risk and business model.

In case 'business model' doesn't seem to translate outside the
commercial world consider the Mid Staffs hospital trust failure
as reported in the Francis inquiry:

> *The overarching value and principle of the NHS Constitution*
> *should be that patients are put first, and everything done by the*
> *NHS and everyone associated with it should be informed by*
> *this ethos.*[9]

We can have an argument that this quote from the inquiry is
talking about culture, but actually it sounds like the top line of a
business model to me. Contrast it to the model the board actually
pursued:

*The Trust prioritised its finances and its Foundation Trust application over its quality of care, and failed to put patients at the centre of its work.*[10]

This report from the 2013 inquiry was followed by similar comment in a Care Quality Commission report into another NHS Foundation Trust in 2014:

*Patient experience was not at the heart of everything that was done at the trust. We witnessed a mixture of 'firefighting' and learned helplessness from frontline staff and an executive team that had focused on financial improvement.*[11]

These are two examples of business models supposedly centred on patient care that became lost in a strategy focused on financial objectives. The strategy may well have converted a budget allocation into headcount, and then ensured that headcount was strictly enforced. The missing question appears to have been how was this done? What assumption of care standards was built into the model under these headcount strictures?

Both of these examples would be in the top left of the four boxes.

The charity Kids Company had an altogether different problem with its business model. Its collapse led to an inquiry by a House of Commons committee which observed that:

*Primary responsibility for Kids Company's collapse rests with the charity's Trustees.*[12]

The report goes on to say that trustees repeatedly ignored auditors' clear warnings about Kids Company's precarious finances and that: *it was run financially "on a knife edge".*

The root of the problem was what the committee described as the charity's operating model, effectively its business model. In setting out to meet its aim to provide practical, emotional and educational support to vulnerable children and young people the charity had adopted a policy of being 'demand-led':

> *Kids Company ran a demand-led operating model, which enabled young people to refer themselves to the charity. The charity's central premise was that no child should be turned away.*[13]

Unfortunately, anyone self-referring was not sponsored by a paying institution, such as a local authority. The inquiry summed up the issue thus:

> *Kids Company's demand-led operating model - based on the doctrine that no child should be turned away - carried the constant risk that the charity would not be able to ensure that its commitments would be matched by its resources. The charity's Trustees failed to address this risk. Instead, the Chief Executive and Trustees relied upon wishful thinking and false optimism and became inured to the precariousness of the charity's financial situation.*[14]

I hope this set of examples does enough to convince you that understanding the business model cannot be a superficial activity. Instead it requires NEDs to be diligent and where necessary inquisitorial. It is not possible to contribute to a strategic debate or understand the organisational risks if the position of the firm 'today' is not understood.

If NEDs just ask 'what' money are we making and 'what' cost savings are in hand without asking 'how' and 'why', well I can't emphasise enough the risks they are running.

Once a business model is understood then understanding the risks to that model raises another NED challenge: is the risk management up to snuff. It is therefore to risk management that we go in the second stage of our journey.

1. http://lexicon.ft.com/Term?term=business-model
2. Ibid.
3. Thinking, Fast and Slow by Daniel Kahneman
4. After pooh-poohing the iPhone years ago, Steve Ballmer just praised Apple—Julie Bort Buisness Insider UK—4 November 2016— http://uk.businessinsider.com/steve-ballmer-just-praised-apple-2016-11?op=1
5. The run on the Rock Fifth Report of Session 2007–08—January 2008
6. http://www.thisismoney.co.uk/money/markets/article-1611508/Interview-Northern-Rock-chief-exec-Adam-Applegarth.html—29 June 2007
7. The run on the Rock Fifth Report of Session 2007–08—January 2008
8. House of Commons Treasury Committee
   The run on the Rock Fifth Report of Session 2007–08—January 2008
9. The Mid Staffordshire NHS Foundation Trust Public Inquiry—February 2013
10. Ibid.
11. Heatherwood and Wexham Park Hospitals NHS Foundation Trust Quality Report 1 May 2014
12. House of Commons Public Administration and Constitutional Affairs Committee—The collapse of Kids Company: lessons for charity trustees, professional firms, the Charity Commission, and Whitehall—Fourth Report of Session 2015–16
13. Ibid.
14. Ibid.

# 20

# RISK MANAGEMENT

R isk management is an immense subject and a professional discipline. Sad to say this makes it easy for NEDs to be blind sided with huge risk packs full of acronyms and jargon ridden content. What the heck is a risk appetite and just how different is that from risk tolerance?

It all made me sit back and think: what is it that NEDs need to be on top of, I mean really on top of?

I have landed on a short list of four items:

1. The relationship between impact and probability
2. Stress testing and reverse stress testing
3. Models, algorithms and why white boxes are better than black boxes
4. Operational resilience and cyber

The relationship between impact and probability shown below is the foundation of risk management.

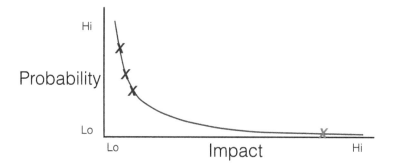

The green crosses plot risks that happen fairly often but the impact of them is pretty low. An example in a retail bank might be a cash difference in a branch, at an insurer: a small claim against a household contents policy for broken crockery, or in a retail store: low value shoplifting.

The red cross is a risk that is highly unlikely to happen, but if it does the impact is devastating. The tsunami that hit Japan in 2011 is an example.

The curve is indicative only, I have drawn it to illustrate one piece of jargon you will come across, *long tail risk*. The red X is in the long tail, it is difficult to predict (probability is so low) and it is difficult to measure (impact is so high). This makes mitigating it, in other words taking actions to reduce one or both of the probability and impact, very hard.

As a simple example you might think of a children's climbing frame which at its highest point has a child ten feet off the ground. Mitigating injury to a child who falls off can be achieved with some sort of soft landing. However, it is a triumph of hope over experience to believe that no child will ever be injured in a fall.

Reducing the height to one foot above the ground will radically reduce the chance of injury, but probably render the climbing frame pretty uninteresting to children. Welcome to risk appetite, what height would you have the frame at?

There is one other point to note at this stage, if a number of the "green cross" risks happen simultaneously or in quick succession they can in combination become a "red cross" risk, as shown below.

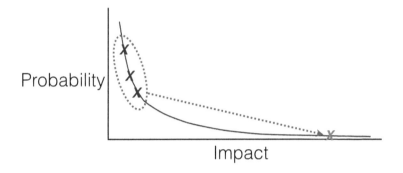

And, "green cross" risks may be an indicator of active failures in the system. This was noted with regards to the tragic sinking of the Herald of Free Enterprise just outside Zeebrugge harbour in 1987:

> *At Zeebrugge, the overworked and undermanned crew of the*
> *Herald of Free Enterprise left harbour with the bow doors*
> *open. This was an oversight caused by a bizarre combination*
> *of active failures (Sheen 1987), but it was also compounded by*
> *strong management pressures to meet the stringent schedule for*
> *the Dover docking.*[1]

The public inquiry headed by Judge Sheen found that the active failures included: understaffing, a routinely overloaded ferry, the need to flood the bow ballast to lower the deck so as to accommodate the low height of the terminal at Zeebrugge and powerful engines that enabled the ferry to pick up speed quickly but created a high bow wave. There were unclear operating instructions to the extent that when the officer responsible for closing the bow doors slept through the departure no-one noticed his absence. Finally, the ferry left late and so quickly cranked its engines up to full speed to meet the pressure to make up time.

Any one of these active failures if they happened in isolation were unlikely to cause the disaster that overtook the ferry. All coinciding was catastrophic.

A request for an indicator light on the bridge to signify if the bow and stern doors were closed had been requested by Captains of the ships. One such request recorded by the inquiry as a *serious memorandum meriting serious thought and attention* elicited these reactions, quoted verbatim by the inquiry:

- *"Do they need an indicator to tell them whether the deck storekeeper is awake and sober? My goodness!!"* ...
- *"Nice but don't we already pay someone!"* ...
- *"Assume the guy who shuts the doors tells the bridge if there is a problem."* ...
- *"Nice!"*

*It is hardly necessary for the Court to comment that these replies display an absence of any proper sense of responsibility*[2].

The request was lost in the bureaucracy of pricing the change but was quickly implemented after the disaster as the inquiry noted:

*That it was simple **is** illustrated by the fact that within a matter of days after the disaster indicator lights were installed in the remaining Spirit class ships and other ships of the fleet*[3].

The inquiry went on to note that:

*As there are lengthy passages in this Report in which there is criticism of the management of the Company, it is only fair to the Company to state at this stage that a new Chair took office only a short time before the disaster and much has been done since to improve the Company's approach to ship management.*[4]

Professor James Reason explains there are two root causes of risks crystallising, the person approach and the system approach.

1. *The person approach focuses on the errors of individuals, blaming them for forgetfulness, inattention, or moral weakness*
2. *The system approach concentrates on the conditions under which individuals work and tries to build defences to avert errors or mitigate their effects ... The basic premise in the system approach is that humans are fallible and errors are to be expected, even in the best organisations.*[5]

This thinking led to a concept known as the Swiss cheese model which is best described graphically:

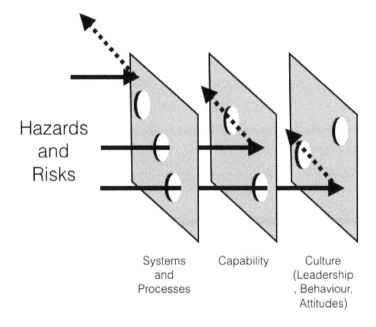

Hazards
and
Risks

| Systems | Capability | Culture |
| and | | (Leadership |
| Processes | | , Behaviour, |
| | | Attitudes) |

*Department of Psychology, University of Manchester, Manchester*
*M13 9PL James Reason professor of psychology—BMJ*
*2000:320:768–70*

What this means is that NEDs overseeing the risk management by their Executives need to expect that people will make
mistakes. With this thinking the *probability* of mistakes
happening can be reduced and, with careful thought plans to
recover from mistakes can be put in place so that *impact* is
reduced.

The Swiss cheese model is effectively a range of preventative
measures such that one failure should not lead to total failure
because another measure protects the system. After the
Zeebrugge disaster there were for instance two measures of
whether the bow and stern doors were closed, the new warning
light and the Officer on duty.

The Zeebrugge disaster is an example of risks that grew

within the organisational system. As described by the Chair of
the public inquiry this went to the top of the ferry owner:

> *The Board of Directors did not appreciate their responsibility*
> *for the safe management of their ships. They did not apply their*
> *minds to the question: What orders should be given for the*
> *safety of our ships? The directors did not have any proper*
> *comprehension of what their duties were.*[6]

1. The contribution of latent human failures to the breakdown of complex
   systems—J. Reason DOI:10.1093/acprof:oso/9780198521914.003.0003
2. MV Herald Of Free Enterprise—Report of Court No. 8074 Formal Investigation Isbn 0 11 550828 7—July 1987
3. Ibid.
4. Ibid.
5. Department of Psychology, University of Manchester, Manchester M13
   9PL James Reason professor of psychology—BMJ 2000:320:768–70
6. MV Herald Of Free Enterprise—Report of Court No. 8074 Formal Investigation Isbn 0 11 550828 7—July 1987

# 21

# STRESS TESTING AND THE FUKUSHIMA QUESTION

S imulating the impact of several risks happening at the same time is a key piece of risk management known as stress testing. What happens to a bank if interest rates, unemployment and inflation rise simultaneously? And a hospital, what happens if a major traffic accident happens on a Saturday night? Accident and emergency is already stretched. Because it is Saturday night many senior staff will be at home. And to top it off the hospital loses its mains power.

I have heard a CEO say to NEDs: *'whilst the impact of the stress is severe don't worry, it is highly unlikely to happen'.* One near disaster and one actual disaster expose the danger of the 'it is unlikely to happen' approach

The actual disaster happened at the Fukushima Daiichi nuclear plant in Japan. The story of the East coast of Japan being hit first by a major earthquake and then by a huge tsunami is well known. As is the terrible and tragic impact on the population. The subsequent explosions and radioactive leaks at the nuclear plant are also well known. Less well understood is the risk management debate that had preceded the tsunami.

*Warnings of possible tsunami risks—the plant is next to one of the world's deepest tectonic trenches, with a history of huge tsunami—were dismissed as "sotei-gai"* [unimaginable events].[1]

The term, sotei-gai, crept into many risk evaluations. This included how high the sea wall protecting the plant should be.

What happened made the height of the sea wall height a pointless debate. The earthquake that preceded and caused the tsunami disabled the plant's primary power supply. Nuclear reactors create a lot of heat and to control this the primary power supply pumped seawater around the reactors. With the primary power knocked out the seawater circulation would have stopped. But, as planned, generators kicked in and cooling continued.

When the tsunami arrived it was 13 meters high and so of course it flowed over the 10 metre high sea wall. Unfortunately the generators were right behind the sea wall. With the generators drowned the vital cooling system failed. The reactors heated up and in the end were rent apart by huge explosions.

*Had the earthquake been an isolated incident* [if there hadn't been an accompanying tsunami], *the plant's generators would have provided backup power until off-site power was restored.*[2]

The Japanese engineers were right to debate the height of the sea wall, but failed to answer the critical question. 'However unlikely it might be, what happens if the sea does come over the wall?' Answering that question would likely have put the generators on a hill behind the plant. This would not have prevented the destruction of the main supply but probably the cooling of the reactors would have continued.

The near disaster happened in 1970. Apollo 13, heading for the moon and at the halfway point of the journey, experienced an onboard explosion. This destroyed its two fuel cells and two oxygen tanks. The reason there were two of each was to provide backup in case of failure.

The initial explosion was inside one of the oxygen tanks. From time to time small pumps in the tanks stirred the liquid oxygen. Unfortunately, unnoticed, one of the pumps had burned out on the ground in testing and when switched on in space it shorted. This caused a spark and given the tank contained liquid oxygen it exploded. This explosion wrecked the adjacent oxygen tank and both fuel cells.

Pre-launch scenario testing by NASA and the crew had involved solving simultaneous faults. And, after the dramatic and successful recovery Swigert, the chief pilot said:

> *"Nobody thought the spacecraft would lose two fuel cells and two oxygen tanks. It couldn't happen. If somebody had thrown that at us in the simulator, we'd have said, 'Come on, you're not being realistic.'"*

These two examples are far away from the risks that cause banks, hospitals and charities to fail. Even so they are bang on the nail in explaining the difficulty of getting stress testing right. The quite understandable temptation to declare 'this is ridiculous, it will never happen'. Along these lines is a comment from Sir Charlie Bean, just before he retired as Deputy Governor at the Bank of England. An institution renowned for taking risk seriously:

*Bean added that he and his colleagues used to brainstorm before the financial crisis about the worst thing that could possibly happen in "My nightmare" sessions: "If any of us had come up with what actually did happen the rest of us would have said, 'You're bonkers'."*[3]

The message for NEDs is always discount Swigert's words *'come on, you're not being realistic'*. Instead, ask the Fukushima question: *'OK, despite how unlikely this appears to be, what would happen if the sea came over the wall?'*

This may well be the difference between survival and failure.

Returning to Northern Rock. The difference of opinion between the FSA and Northern Rock over stress testing is an example of a regulator failing to deal with a firm pushing back.

*Although the Board of Northern Rock undertook some stress testing of its own business model, it proved to have been thoroughly inadequate. It was the responsibility of the Financial Services Authority to ensure that the work of the Board of Northern Rock was sufficient to the task.*[4]

Northern Rock was not an outlier. The FSA was one of many national regulators at the time who instructed banks to stress their business models. Yet, many scenarios banks produced were hardly stresses at all. In numerous cases they were the meteorological equivalent of being asked to prepare for a typhoon, and then producing a plan to cope with a light shower and a bit of a breeze.

This led regulators to ask for reverse stress tests. In other words for boards to work out what would it take for their bank to fail. Directors' reaction to proposed stress tests and then reverse stress tests, led to some severe criticism of the regulators. Exactly the push back regulators have experienced in the past that led to hesitation and, in the end, failure of both the regulator and the bank. It's worth adding that executives who resist stress testing and reverse stress testing raise the reddest of red flags for NEDs.

Remember that question, the best one in risk management: *'OK, despite how unlikely this appears to be, what would happen if the sea came over the wall?'*

Finally, in case anyone feels the need to scoff at sotei-gai, *unimaginable events*, let us not forget Northern Rock:

*The idea of all markets closing to Northern Rock was repeatedly characterised to us by Northern Rock officials as "unforeseeable".*[5]

1. My time in Japan's closed nuclear village—Gregory Clark, July 2016—ft.com   https://www.ft.com/content/1c5fb030-cf37-11e1-a1ae-00144feab-dc0?mhq5j=e3
2. The Fukushima Disaster and Japan's Nuclear Plant Vulnerability in Comparative Perspective—Phillip Y. Lipscy,, Kenji E. Kushida and Trevor Incerti—dx.doi.org/10.1021/es4004813 | Environ. Sci. Technol. 2013, 47, 6082−6088
3. As reported in the Evening Standard 21 May 2014.
4. House of Commons Treasury Committee: The Run On The Rock—Fifth Report of Session 2007–08
5. Ibid.

# 22

# MODELS, ALGORITHMS AND WHY WHITE BOXES ARE BETTER THAN BLACK BOXES

The next stage of our risk journey concerns the impact of technology, particularly the advance of complex decision making models. This is Warren Buffett on the subject:

*Indeed, the stupefying losses in mortgage-related securities came in large part because of flawed, history-based models used by salesmen, rating agencies and investors. These parties looked at loss experience over periods when home prices rose only moderately and speculation in houses was negligible. They then made this experience a yardstick for evaluating future losses. They blissfully ignored the fact that house prices had recently skyrocketed, loan practices had deteriorated and many buyers had opted for houses they couldn't afford. In short, universe "past" and universe "current" had very different characteristics. But lenders, government and media largely failed to recognise this all-important fact.*[1]

This illustrates the role of the NED which is to understand and where necessary challenge the underlying model assumptions. In the example described by Buffett the key assumptions were that previous calm markets would always continue and house prices would never fall. Buffett went on to stress the importance of scepticism. When he talks here of the investors remember he is a major investor in Berkshire Hathaway but what he says applies just as well to NEDs:

> *Investors* [NEDs] *should be sceptical of history-based models. Constructed by a nerdy-sounding priesthood using esoteric terms such as beta, gamma, sigma and the like, these models tend to look impressive. Too often, though, investors* [NEDs] *forget to examine the assumptions behind the symbols. Our advice: Beware of geeks bearing formulas.*[2]

Models are here to stay. Competition in business is now too complex, with markets moving too fast and data volumes too massive to be managed otherwise. The key for NEDS in exercising oversight over models is to question, critique and above all understand the assumptions that have been used from which all the complex maths is derived. This does not mean being an expert in modelling or an accomplished mathematician.

The idea is that NEDs understand the key basis of the model design and what significant assumptions underly this design. It is also important to know where the model stops working and if 'expert judgement' is applied who's expert judgement? All models have limits in their effectiveness, so what are the significant limitations?

A simple example would be a credit model that has been created for prime mortgages. It has been well done, being based on good design and extensive amounts of quality data. However, let us say this is then used to model the entrance to a segment of the sub-prime mortgage market for which the firm has no relevant data. Any output from the model used in this way is now suspect if not downright wrong.

An analogy would be to say that since the family car can tow a small trailer on a metalled road it is also suitable for towing a large trailer fully loaded with hay bales across a muddy field.

Model sign off and use typifies a general challenge all boards face which is to get the balance between detail and big picture right. Put another way, where is it wrong to ask for detail and where is it wrong not to ask for detail?

Let me try and help describe the issue of computer led decision making by telling the story of how I was taught to lend. Joining a big bank straight from school led over time to being let loose lending money. Now, bearing in mind in the early 1970's there were no desktop computers, no credit scorecards and all records were typed with copies produced via carbon paper, you might wonder how the bank achieved any kind of consistent approach to lending money. Well, we were guided by training, by a senior manager overseeing our lending and by a mnemonic. The mnemonic was CCCPARTS still stamped on my memory today:

C - *Character*, is this an honest person?
C - *Capability*, is the person good at what they do?
C - *Capital*, how much is the bank lending versus the borrower?
P - *Purpose*, is it legal, valid and worthwhile?
A - *Amount*, has the borrower considered all eventualities?
R - *Repayment*, how and when will the bank be repaid?
T - *Terms*, fees and interest rate
S - *Security*, what has the borrower pledged in case of default?

There was a lot more behind the scenes of course. For instance, *Capital* was strictly controlled, the bank would not lend more than 50% as a matter of course because then the bank owned the project, it became in effect an equity investor. Another example is *Amount*. My manager drummed into me that borrowers had a habit of underestimating what they needed because of looking on the bright side and fearing to ask for too much. In hindsight I was being taught stress testing: look at the cashflow and imagine the income arrives two months late, now how much does the borrower need?

What on earth am I telling you this for? Well, whilst a sketchy description I suggest that you now understand how we used to lend and it doesn't take a moment to work out this approach still works today. Many small firms 'manually' under-write loans and where they do then a variation of training, expe-rienced oversight and their version of CCCPARTS will be in use.

The big challenge is and always has been information. What do you really know about the customer and what information characterises a bad loan and a good loan? When I started out local knowledge, experience and interview skills were the keys to gathering the right information and to understanding the difference between good and bad. This challenge began to be met in a different way in the early 1990s. Computer systems were built that modelled the information collected using statis-tical analysis and began to scientifically differentiate between good and bad.

Proxies began to be used. Ask yourself how a modeller meets the first C, Character, how does a model measure honesty? It will have to be a metric, it can't be judgement, there needs to be a measure. Perhaps it is no missed loan repayments and no court actions against the potential borrower.

Then the second C, how to measure competence. How do I know if my plumber is a good plumber. Maybe there is website feedback from the plumber's customers which can be used, if not maybe we fall back on no missed repayments and no court actions.

I hope you get the drift. Models can be mathematical wonders but the killer question is what assumptions did the modeller make to try and get the model to mimic a real life deci-sion maker.

In essence over the last quarter century we have moved from

an understandable underwriting process based on experience to the complexities of mathematically 'precise' statistical modelling as portrayed below.

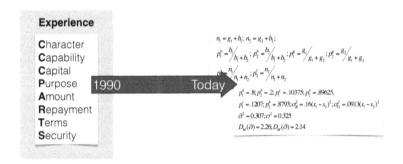

In the 1970s a non-banker NED on the board could grasp the essence of lending based on CCCPARTS. Today, the question is how can the NED understand the credit risk model, bearing in mind if it isn't understood then the NED is sat on top of a black box. This question has three answers, two of which are wrong.

The first wrong answer is that this is too complex for the board and therefore faith has to be placed in the experts who have written the formulae and algorithms that drive decisions output from the model. It's wrong because this is the black box approach.

The second wrong answer is for NEDs to be coached on the maths, to become statisticians and to get into the detail of challenging the formulae. This is also wrong because it is implausible to expect any board to be coached into a comprehension of complex maths, besides which this is not what they are there for.

The third and right answer is for the NEDs to have explained to them the assumptions on which it is built: what customer segments will it work for, what won't it work for? What is the riskiest lending the model will allow, presented as a description of the customer, product or security? At what point does the model not work? Why have the assumptions been made?

Although it might be a back to the future moment, explaining a lending model in terms of CCCPARTS gets to the essence of what is needed.

I have used lending as an example but of course the range of models being deployed today is growing. Everything from Chat-Bots in contact centres to analysis of medical scans. The buzz words of today: Big Data, Artificial Intelligence and Neural Networks seem designed to baffle the honest NED and Trustee. However, the principles remain the same: check the assumptions and check the output in real world terms.

A good approach for any NED is to regard all models as a three part process: input, process and output. With that thinking the actions become clear.

1. Input - what are the assumptions that have been made?
2. Process - what is the framework by which the complex maths have been developed? Has this been validated externally by other experts? Will it degrade over time and if so how long before it needs renewing?
3. Output - in simple language what is happening

It is through checking outcomes that NEDs learn about the real world impact of the model. Is it achieving the business result? Is it fair? Is it biased?

The bias of models that have taught themselves through Machine Learning is well known. This arises because the machine learns from historic data within which may be embedded unfairness and bias. There is for instance the example of the CV filtering system for IT staff that rejected female applicants. No-one designed this in it was simply the machine learning, from historic CVs, there were few female applicants.

In overseeing models NEDs need to be aware that there are

in effect two communities using two different languages. One community, the board, are focused on commercial success and a viable and sustainable business model implicit within which is that customers are treated fairly. The language used to describe how the model works ought to address these fundamentals and not be deeply technical. The problem is that the second community is exactly that, technical. The translation of the work being done from technospeak to English is as important as the technical work itself.

That this problem is not limited to banks is clearly evident from the debacle at Volkswagen where cars passed diesel emissions tests by cheating. This is the initial press coverage:

> *In 2005, VW decided to sell a lot of diesel cars in the US. Sometime later, a group "whose identity is still being determined" — but below management board level — changed the engines' software, allowing them to pass emissions tests while violating emissions rules on the road.*[3]

This brings home the responsibility and accountability of the management and board. If the changes were made 'below management board level' then this begs a few questions: how were the changes allowed? What were the checks and balances that should have caught this kind of activity and why if they existed did they not work? If they did not exist, then why was this? If the organisational system allowed this key decision to be made with no oversight, then as Reason argued it is a *system approach* issue rather than *person approach*. However, it is the person being blamed.

The board has a responsibility that goes beyond understanding the assumptions underpinning individual models. It must include the framework, described in plain English, through which models and algorithms are created, used and changed.

The responsibility of Executive Directors is to facilitate the translation by the analysts out of 'nerdy quant' language and into the plain English the NEDs can understand. It is particularly important the output of the models is clear.

- This kind of borrower (income, job, security) would be turned down
- This kind of market trade could take place and our terms & conditions are met (for example, we say we are not preferring some clients over others and we don't)
- This sample of scans reveal no problems for the patient

I am not for a moment saying that NEDs have to engage with every model in the business. As usual they are faced with priorities. However, NEDs need to have a framework in place that catches the high profile models and quickly reveals models whose output is unfair, biased or just plain wrong. This is a growing feature of businesses and so the need for NED oversight is increasingly important. A foremost thinker about the impact of technology on decision making is Professor Joanna Bryson who summarises neatly this whole chapter:

*... it is critical to remember that what we are holding account-able is not machines themselves, but the people who build, own, or operate them—including any who alter their operation through assault on their cybersecurity. What we need to govern is the human application of technology: what we need to oversee are human processes of development, testing, operation, and monitoring*[4].

1. Berkshire Hathaway Inc.—2008 Annual Report
2. Berkshire Hathaway Inc.—2008 Annual Report
3. Volkswagen: mind and body - FT.com
   04/03/2016
4. The Artificial Intelligence of the Ethics of Artificial Intelligence: An Introductory Overview for Law and Regulation—Joanna J. Bryson July 28, 2019

# 23

# OPERATIONAL RESILIENCE AND CYBER SECURITY

W hy twin operational resilience (OpRes) and cyber security (Cyber) together? Basically because defence against Cyber is utterly dependant on OpRes which is why this chapter title is OpRes and Cyber and not the other way round. The best way I can explain this is to quote Lyndon Nelson an Executive Director of the Bank of England:

> *We have seen that operational failures can happen and unless something dramatically changes we can expect them to happen again. Cyber adds a further sense of urgency as incidents are human led, intelligent and deliberately exploitative. Hence the fact that regulators and firms have been pushing operational resilience up the agenda[1].*

OpRes is not a new idea, it has been around for at least thirty years. However, the current pace of change to the environment in which firms in all sectors operate is raising the pressures on OpRes considerably.

Comparing today's environment with, say only twenty years ago, firms are contending with these increased OpRes risks:

- use of outsourcing and third parties
- smartphone apps
- Bring Your Own Device
- The constant need to patch and update systems
- the changing definition of privacy
- cloud computing
- the difficulty of modernising legacy systems
- more regulators and more intrusive regulation
- the globalisation and professionalising of crime
- state sponsored attacks

This is nowhere near an exhaustive list but it does help to set out that the scale of OpRes is much wider than Cyber.

The issue of language is again all important. Asking is OpRes the same as Operational Risk is a bit like the Risk Appetite versus Risk Tolerance debate. The main point is that NEDs need to know what is meant in their firm. If either description focuses just on Cyber then the broader question about risks beyond cyber is not being answered.

There is a generational issue here as well. The generation many of today's NEDs grew up in spent its youth with no personal technology at all and where Cyber was a particular sort of villain in Doctor Who. The youngest generation in the NED's firm has grown up in a world of personal technology. As was put to me by one NED, *when it comes to technology, few if any of the board have personal experience to draw on*. In all other risk areas: credit, market, mortality, etc., there will be experience to some degree or other around the boardroom.

So this is temporary then and when the old generation finally retire boards will be populated increasingly by tech savvy NEDs. I doubt it. I suspect that the younger generation will always be one technological step ahead of the older generation. Which is all OK because that is not the issue. As we discussed earlier when looking at algorithms and models, it's not about the maths or the technology, it is about the outcomes and that is where the wisdom of the NED is applied.

As an example, one NED told me that in order for the cyber debate to gain traction in her firm the board decreed that all board papers had to include a section on cyber security, explaining the impact of the subject matter on cyber security present and cyber security future. This inevitably gave cyber security a focus right the way across and through the executive. This is NED wisdom in action.

Another example is outsourcing and a subset of outsourcing, cloud computing.

Outsourcing decisions are business decisions not technical decisions. Why is this a better idea than retaining the processes and technology within our business? What new risks emerge from this transfer to third parties? What old risks do we hope to see mitigated? Will we lose valuable knowledge that we may need in the future?

Taking cloud computing. Firstly, be clear that the definition of cloud computing is: 'your data and processes are on someone else's computer'. That may be a good thing:

- reduced running costs
- no need to budget for future capital expenditure to update data centres
- no need to protect networks and data centres from cyber attack
- flexibility of processing power and data storage

However, the NED's firm is still accountable to its customers if the outsourcing supplier suffers a data breach or a systems outage. The identification of lower running costs should be fairly straightforward and the avoided capital investment capable of estimation. Data protection and systems resilience from outage are much more difficult matters to quantify.

NEDs need to know the executives have considered and gained answers to a whole raft of questions such as:

1. does the contract with the provider allow for our own audits to take place?
2. how easy will it be to transfer the data and processes to another provider?
3. what happens if the provider is bought by another company, what if that company is based in a jurisdiction that is questionable?
4. how fast will the provider advise of breakdowns or cyber attacks?

Take number 2 down a level of detail: a firm has real problems if in practice it can't move its business when the provider is found to be offering a lamentable service.

I'm sure you will have noticed these are not technical questions.

All of the above applies to any operation that is outsourced to a third party. Cloud is simply an example.

Whether or not operations are outsourced cyber security should be top of mind for NEDs. The wrong cyber question is how to prevent an attack happening, because you won't be able to. Instead the question is: how can we reduce the chance of our systems being compromised, our data being locked in a ransomware attack or stolen? And crucially, when it happens, how do we recover?

There must of course be investment in capability to withstand attack on systems but it is too easy to make this investment and to be assured that all is now well. Think of it this way, your metaphorical sea wall is now a robust 10 metres high. Ask the question: 'OK, crazy as it may seem to ask this, what happens if the sea does come over the wall? And, if it does, what do we do about it?'

Staying with the ocean, the global shipping group Maersk provides a sobering lesson of what can happen from a major outage, caused in their case by a malware infection. Having succumbed to the *Wannacry* attack in 2017 Maersk was then hit again by the *NotPetya* malware. During the recovery Maersk employees were manually logging shipping containers using local spreadsheets and paper and pen. There was uncertainty about ship arrivals and departures and customer's found difficulty knowing where their freight was.

*Some of the containers ...sent on Maersk's ships that day* [when the malware hit] *would remain lost in cargo yards and ports around the world for the next three months.*[2]

*The NotPetya outbreak had a huge impact on Maersk - the firm apparently lost between $250m and $300m as a direct result of the attack, and was forced to conduct its business manually without the aid of IT systems while the damage was repaired.*[3]

There is a twofold answer to Cyber, firstly: to be able, as far as possible, to withstand attacks and secondly: to be able to recover as quickly and completely as possible. I will quote Lyndon Nelson again:

*... the cyber attacker like a liquid has found every crack and gap in firms' defences and settled at the level where there are the fewest controls. These can be related to gaps in process, or technology, people, skills and awareness.*[4]

I mentioned earlier the globalisation and professionalisation of crime. The most professional criminal gangs will be running projects every bit as complex and professionally managed as the projects NEDs are used to seeing in their own organisations. The proceeds of crime, either stealing money or holding data to ransom is massive. The motivation may also be to steal intellectual property or to cause operational confusion and disruption. There are plenty of 'threat actors' who are state sponsored.

Whilst all this feels bad enough there is the threat of insider action to weaken or dodge defences. This can be a member of staff who makes a mistake through that phishing e-mail or someone with a grudge against the firm or a downright criminal.

I vividly remember the time one of my departments recruited a person who worked diligently and well and after a two year period became a first line manager. Then, in a week, we lost £1mn as funds which should have been remitted to other banks in the UK went to another country. After a frantic investigation we discovered our culprit, a drug user being manipulated by an organised crime gang. The person went to prison, the crime gang was never found and I had a very tricky meeting with the Audit Committee explaining why my controls had been so hopeless.

The subsequent audit investigation into this incident also highlighted the recruitment process which, because the person started as a temporary contractor, had not been as rigorously applied. The rigour was not picked up when the transfer from temp to permanent took place after a year. You can see the Swiss Cheese at work here: the perfect alignment of the recruitment hole with the process control hole and the cultural hole of instinctively trusting a colleague who has been around for a while.

Now, imagine the same circumstances, but the new starter is coding in the technology department and after two years becomes a systems administrator.

I will close this section by quoting Lyndon Nelson one more time:

> I would like our firms to be on a WAR footing: withstand: absorb: recover.[5]

Withstand the attack, as far as possible. Absorb the attack, by rapidly closing down and isolating the attacked part of the business. Recover from the attack with as little disruption as possible.

The NED contribution is to make sure the Executives are taking action. That they have thought through and practised exercises ready for the unfortunate day when the sea does come over the wall. Getting this kind of outlook to be business as usual requires in many cases a cultural shift and so it is to culture that we go next.

1. 'Operational resilience in financial services: time to act' report launch— Speech given by Lyndon Nelson, Deputy CEO & Executive Director, Prudential Regulation Authority
2. The Untold Story of NotPetya, The Most Devastating Cyberattack In History—Mike McQuade and Andy Greenberg—Wired Magazine 22 August 2018
3. ITPRO—Adam Shepherd 26 January 2018 http://www.itpro.co.uk/cyber-attacks/30393/maersk-rebuilt-hefty-it-infrastructure-a-mere-10-days-after-notpetya-attack
4. Resilience and continuity in an interconnected and changing world – speech by Lyndon Nelson. Given at the 20th Annual OperationalRisk Europe conference, London June 2018—https://www.bankofengland.co.uk/speech/2018/lyndon-nelson-regulatory-keynote-address-at-opsrisk-europe
5. Ibid.

# 24

# CULTURE

There is so much written about culture that I admit I became bogged down, it all began to feel a bit 'over-thought'.

Attempts to define culture often include words such as values, ethics, morals and standards. Whilst these are indisputably woven into culture there is so little agreement on what they mean that one person's values can be someone else's morals. And that's before you get to 'tone from the top', which apparently is so important it has more definitions than eskimos have words for snow.

As a result of searching for a simpler perspective I was reminded of a seminar I attended in the 1990s led by John Adair[1], who was then visiting Professor of Leadership at the University of Exeter. Early in the session John asked the syndicate, there were nine of us, 'what one word sums up leadership'. I ask you to ponder on that for a minute before reading on. We pondered on it for most of the afternoon without coming close and in the end John said 'the word is influence because if you cannot influence others you cannot lead'. Twenty odd years later I found this somewhat forgotten moment coming back to me as I thought about culture. As influence is to leadership I wondered, 'what' is to culture? I wondered this because as you know I want to know what it is I'm supposed to do at five past nine on a rainy Monday morning.

Explaining values, mindsets and other hidden aspects of culture doesn't help explain what it is that needs to be done. Homely phrases like, 'it's the way we do things around here' and 'it's what people do when the boss isn't around' don't help much either.

My problem is how? How do you get the way we do things around here to be a good way and how do you get people to do those good things when the boss isn't around?

Salvation lay in one word that kept cropping up in my research, that word is behaviour. It appears that a very measurable cultural output is how people behave.

The Financial Reporting Council in the UK completed their first piece of work on corporate culture in July 2016[2], this contains quotes from experienced directors and one stood out:

*What counts is the actual behaviour of the organisation and its top people. This is far more significant than a hundred statements about a company's culture or its ethical policy.*

Well, hear hear to that.

A final test is to ask how most people describe whether a culture is good or bad. Invariably the descriptions are behaviours.

Reflecting again on John Adair's leadership seminar I conclude it is behaviour that is to culture as influence is to leadership. And, if you think about it, being asked to *lead a culture change* is open to interpretation. However, being asked to *influence a change in behaviour* brings much more focus to the issue at hand. It sets out an obvious pair of questions for a start: 'what are the behaviours we see today and what would we like to see tomorrow'? Followed by: 'how to go from today to tomorrow?'.

Explaining that behaviour is the measurable end product of culture is all well and good but begs an important question, what is it that drives behaviour? Furthermore, can we exercise control over this so as to be able to influence changes in behaviour, and thus lead a culture change?

If behaviour is the end product, what is the start point? Well, I don't think it is values, ethics, morals and standards. The start point is what is the point? What is the point of what we are doing, in other words 'what is our *Purpose*?'

---

1. John Adair is one of the world's leading authorities on leadership and leadership development. Over a million managers worldwide have taken part in the Action-Centred Leadership programmes he pioneered. http://www.johnadair.co.uk
2. Corporate Culture and the Role of Boards. https://www.frc.org.uk/Our-Work/Publications/Corporate-Governance/Corporate-Culture-and-the-Role-of-Boards-Report-0.pdf

# 25

# PURPOSE AND BEHAVIOUR

Asking 'what is our *Purpose?*' is not without its own ambiguity. Setting out *Purpose* often leads to a grandly worded Vision or a collection of aspirational objectives. Almost certainly at least one of values, ethics, morals and standards will be referenced, but often what is missing is the answer to the question, what is the point?

What is the point of this organisation, this company, partnership or charity? A better and tougher question to ask is what would society miss if our organisation did not exist? This is the true point of an organisation.

Asking what society would miss can face leaders with some tricky moments if the organisational *Purpose* in practice is to take unfair advantage of others. It also creates problems if the *Purpose* espoused by the governing body and senior leaders is not recognised by the workforce, who on a day to day basis in the front line see something quite different.

Therefore, I am a firm believer that *Purpose* is the start point of culture.

Once *Purpose* is debated, clarified and set out by the organisation's governing body then the behavioural standards that the workforce has to deliver against to achieve the *Purpose* can be agreed. Whether these standards are defined in terms of morals, ethics or values is somewhat immaterial as long as it is clear what behaviour is acceptable and what isn't. Once all of this is understood then what comes next is communication, in as clear a way as possible, to the workforce and the outside world.

I sum up this work of the governing body, this collection of *Purpose*, Behavioural Standards and Communication, as the tone from the top.

At which point I will give you my view on this well loved phrase. People enjoy playing endlessly with it but seldom think about how it works. Additionally, you get pejorative derivatives like 'the muttering from the middle', with added spice when middle management doing the muttering are described as 'permafrost'.

Permafrost and muttering are descriptions used when 'the top' hasn't thought hard enough about how its 'tone' actually works. Thus, in it not working, because enough thought has not been given to the *Purpose* and Behavioural Standards, it is handy to find scapegoats. It has always amazed me that middle management, the cadre who often carry an organisation and are essential to its behaviour can be labelled 'permafrost', very often by their own senior leaders.

The tone from the top appears as step 1 in the diagram below.

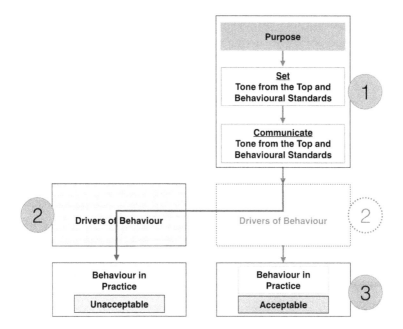

You will see that step 3, which is what happens in practice, is not a given just because the tone from the top is clearly thought through and communicated. This is because the tone from the top merely sets out what is wanted, of itself it has little power to make the required behaviour actually happen in practice. It has to be supported by congruent drivers of behaviour.

If the drivers of behaviour are not aligned with the *Purpose* then the behaviours that will be seen in practice will be at odds with what is set out in the tone from the top. This is shown by the red arrow. Getting drivers of behaviour aligned with the tone from the top such that steps 1 and 2 are lined up is the only way to get the right behaviours in practice at step 3.

The drivers of behaviour must be aligned with the stated purpose because the true test of tone from the top is behaviour. No matter how well defined and communicated the tone from the top is if behaviour is poor then so is the tone from the top.

When drivers of behaviour are not aligned with *Purpose* it is not surprising *t*hat surveys (such as the UK Banking Standards Board and www.glassdoor.com) find employees saying:

- I do not always trust what our senior leaders say
- Sometimes I have to trade ethics for results
- Our strategy is unclear

As a simple exercise imagine the tale of a salesforce with a *Purpose* to provide unbiased and excellent advice to customers. The required behavioural standards have been thought through and set out and clear communication with the work force has taken place.

The *Purpose,* unbiased and excellent advice, relies on the workforce of advisers establishing the customers' need and then looking across the range of available products to find what mix best satisfies that. This has been supported with a thorough training programme.

However, in practice, the advisers are rewarded for selling a few highly profitable products and not so well rewarded for selling the remainder. Thus the advisers' financial incentive, one important driver of behaviour, is not congruent with the *Purpose*. As a result the advice becomes biased and is not in the slightest bit excellent.

The seminal academic paper on incentives written over forty years ago rejoices in the title: *On The Folly of Rewarding A, While Hoping For B.*[1] In a nutshell, if the tone from the top talks eloquently about B but senior leaders reward A then please expect A not B.

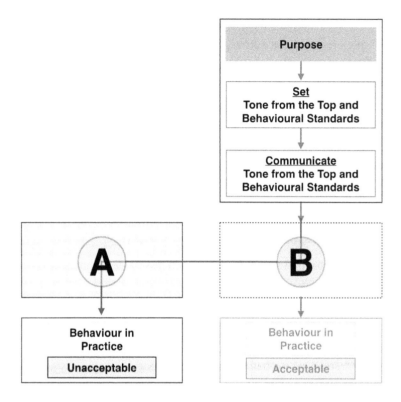

This is destructive not only to customers but also to the organisation.

It is destructive to the customers because in our salesforce tale their needs are not being met, indeed their interests far from being looked after by the advisers may well be harmed.

It is destructive to the organisation in several ways. Firstly, if the reward system is designed to maximise profit then this can only be at the expense of the customer, and an organisation that rips off anyone has a looming problem. This is because as we saw in business models, it will be found out in the end by an investigative journalist, an investigative regulator or a whistle-blower. The resulting sanctions of fines and customer redress, heavy though these may be, only add to the reputational damage suffered by the organisation.

As destructive is the impact on the organisation's culture. People are being encouraged by the organisation to behave in the wrong way. All the while hearing and seeing a communication, externally and internally, extolling the organisation's virtuous approach to unbiased advice and excellence. It is the cultural equivalent of writing in large friendly letters over the door, 'it's OK around here to rip people off'.

The cultural damage extends to the trust the workforce place in senior leaders. After all, it is pretty dishonest to say one thing and then encourage quite the reverse.

Further damage is done when the advisers in our tale who cannot cope with ripping customers off leave. Replacement advisers recruited to fill the gaps will realise they have to make the same judgement: 'am I prepared to rip people off?' If the answer is no then they also will leave. If the answer is yes, then an increasing number of bad apple advisers will eventually produce a very bad barrel indeed. Of course, the barrel was always going to go bad the minute the organisation's leadership decided it was OK to say one thing but pay the workforce to do the opposite.

The final cultural destruction, when the organisation has been found out, is if advisers are sanctioned and not the governing body.

A clear *Purpose* will only succeed if it is underpinned by drivers of behaviour that reinforce its delivery. By definition this will deliver a tone from the top that is honest, reliable and competent, the result of which is a trustworthy organisation. Sir Adrian Cadbury pointed to this:

> The 1992 corporate governance report said: 'It is important that all employees should know what standards of conduct are expected of them. We regard it as good practice for boards of directors to draw up codes of ethics or statements of business practice and to publish them both internally and externally.'[2]

I agree with this but note that the link to what drives behaviour is not made.

Given the drivers of behaviour are so important can we identify them? I believe so.

Since you can't get the required behaviours without communicating the tone from the top in stage 1 *effective communication* is an obvious driver.

Another candidate from our advisers tale is incentives. These come in two forms, financial and non-financial, and so *incentives* is another driver.

Key to any endeavour is trust in the leadership of the organisation, people need to be able to believe in their leaders. If leaders are seen to say one thing and do another, especially if what they do or say is contrary to the *Purpose* then expect at best confusion and at worst cynicism: 'if the boss doesn't care why should I?'. Therefore *trust in senior leaders* is a driver too and we return again to Sir Adrian Cadbury for confirmation:

*Boards, therefore, have the dual role of framing codes of conduct and of living by them.*[3]

The final driver is *decision making* because culture forms and develops as people throughout the firm judge management on management's judgements. Which is a sentence you may want to re-read.

In watching the decisions made by the CEO and board, people throughout the organisation will look for two things: do decisions turn out well and if they don't what happens? This is because people like working for winners but recognise that not all decisions do turn out well. But, if the decision that turns out in a disappointing way or downright badly is not owned by the decision maker, and others carry the can, then this behaviour is seen for what it is and honesty bites the dust.

The lack of responsibility assumed by senior people has been one of the enduring features of the 2007/8 bank failures. It is therefore no great leap to understand why popular trust in bankers has disappeared.

What follows now is an explanation of these four drivers of behaviour:

1. Trustworthiness of senior leaders
2. Communications
3. Decision making
4. Incentives, financial and non-financial

The overarching point is that all four need to align if behaviour is to be what the governing body envisages will deliver the *Purpose* of the organisation.

The failings at Mid Staffs NHS Trust serve as a stark warning to any board regarding culture which flows from the top:

> *The Trust's culture was one of self promotion rather than critical analysis and openness. This can be seen from the way the Trust approached its Foundation Trust application ... ... its inaccurate self declaration of its own performance. It took false assurance from good news, and yet tolerated or sought to explain away bad news.*[4]

Culture is not a headwind to success, it's a tail wind, but getting culture to be a tail wind is way beyond just ticking boxes. Culture is not passive it is active. Therefore the shaping of culture by the firm's leadership cannot be passive it also has to be active.

1. On the Folly of Rewarding A, While Hoping for B—Author(s): Steven Kerr—Source: The Academy of Management Journal, Vol. 18, No. 4 (Dec., 1975), pp. 769-783
2. Cadbury, Adrian. Corporate Governance and Chairship: A Personal View. OUP Oxford.
3. Ibid.
4. Report of the Mid Staffordshire NHS Foundation Trust Public Inquiry—February 2013—Robert Francis QC

# 26

# TRUST AND TRUSTWORTHINESS

*Once lost, trust cannot be restored. We would like to wind the clock back and ask to be trusted again, but we cannot eradicate the word or action. They hang like a judgment against which there is no appeal.*[1]

I n looking at the four drivers of behaviour I am going to start with Trustworthiness. I start here because if we have no trust in our senior leaders then it doesn't really matter how good the communication, incentives and decision making are. There is therefore a hierarchy to the four behavioural drivers as shown here:

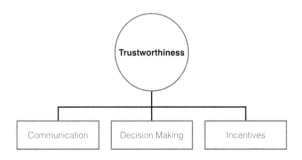

In starting with trustworthiness we need to be clear what we mean. The philosopher Baroness Onora O'Neil explains the relationship between 'trust' and 'trustworthy' in this way:

> *... trust is something that other people place in you, it's not something you can create or demand. What you can create however is 'trustworthiness'. People will place trust in you if you are trustworthy.*[2]

Banks in particular, but also corporations generally, are often accused of a lack of trust. In fact what they lack is trustworthiness and because of that people will not place trust in them. Baroness O'Neil sets out three dimensions of trustworthiness: honesty, reliability and competence[3] and points out having an aim of more trust is wrong:

> *The aim is to have more trust. Well frankly, I think that's a stupid aim. It's not what I would aim at. I would aim to have more trust in the trustworthy but not in the untrustworthy. In fact, I aim positively to try not to trust the untrustworthy. And I think, of those people who, for example, placed their savings with the very aptly named Mr. Madoff, who then made off with them, and I think of them, and I think, well, yes, too much trust. More trust is not an intelligent aim in this life. Intelligently placed and intelligently refused trust is the proper aim.*[4].

It's pretty clear that the CEO and board need to be seen as trustworthy if they are to gain the trust of the workforce. This is an essential first step if they are to create an organisation that is also seen as trustworthy.

Trust is right at the heart of tone from the top. This is particularly so with regards to the stated purpose of the organisation. If there is any sort of gap between the stated purpose in stage 1 and the drivers in stage 2 then this will be interpreted by the workforce as a lack of honesty. It will also likely deliver a different purpose in practice, not at all what customers expected.

In determining the stated purpose of the firm the board exposes itself both internally and externally to being measured up for trustworthiness. The only difference is that the internal assessment will happen first.

Think for a moment of the board that agrees with its new CEO that the organisation will chart a fresh strategy of placing the customer at the heart of everything. The previous strategy of maximising profit is now secondary to the customer. When this decision is communicated internally the workforce will immediately begin to pass judgement on it and thus on the CEO and the board. If employees know that through lack of past investment products and service are poor then they will look for tangible indications of what is going to change.

More central will be the stoical wait by everyone for the first test. When the new strategy demands at some point that profit has to be foregone, will this happen?

We have already seen this in action with the Mid Staffs NHS example where poor patient care arose because financial control and hitting targets came first despite the clear ethos of the NHS.

The most toxic outcome of a failure of trustworthiness is not just that staff do not trust the board and management but that corrosively over time staff begin not to care. If the board don't care why should they? This is just as applicable to industrial scale miss-selling as it is to hospital care.

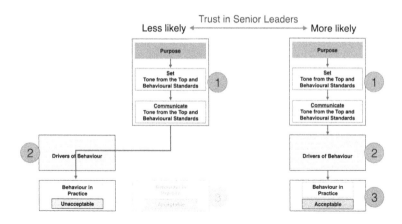

The congruence of the three stage model with all three stages aligned is an essential part of the trustworthiness of the CEO, board and therefore the organisation.

Before turning to the next driver, communication, let me finish with a quote from another philosopher, Friedrich Nietzche, which perfectly sums up this section on trust:

> *"I'm not upset that you lied to me, I'm upset that from now on I can't believe you."*

1. Firm Commitment: Why the corporation is failing us and how to restore trust in it—Colin Mayer
2. Baroness Nora O'Neil, TED talk: https://www.ted.com/talks/onora_o_neil-l_what_we_don_t_understand_about_trust
3. Ibid.
4. Ibid

# 27

# COMMUNICATION AND THE UGLY TRUTH

A bell weather for all leaders is whether your workforce, at all levels, is willing to say: *"boss, we have a problem, the ugly truth is ..."*. And then they tell you the ugly truth. In my experience that conversation is worth diamonds and a major indicator your organisation's culture is healthy. It is built on trust, our first driver, and on communication, our second.

The communication challenge is how to deliver in both directions, *from* the board and *to* the board. The figure below stylises this:

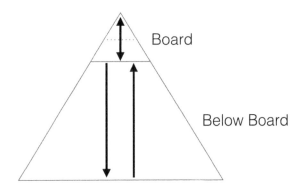

The NEDs delegate communication below board to executive management and particularly the CEO. However, the NEDs must still oversee this important activity to check it is producing desired results.

One might ask what could possibly go wrong? Of course the answer is obvious, life and communication is not simple. Think friction when thinking of communication. The further a message has to travel the more friction applies and the less likely the message is to get there unchanged. Or even at all. All sorts of barriers exist which transform the diagram above to that below:

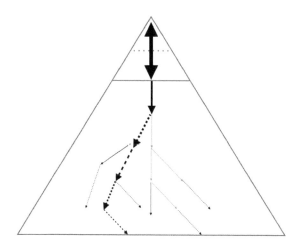

Typically these barriers include:

- Different geographies
- Shift working
- Language
- Differing national cultures
- New starters versus old hands
- Integration of people in a new acquisition
- Part time workers
- Executive rivalry, information is power

- Executives not organising communication properly
- Executives not communicating clearly
- Executives not communicating at all
- Executives protecting their own reputations

On top of this the fork-lift drivers in the warehouse will appreciate a different sort of message to the lawyers in the General Counsel's office.

Planning communication has to be meticulous, if it is off the cuff it will be off message too.

It is not only downwards communication where friction applies. It is also a problem for upwards communication, with a very notable wrinkle. The diagram below shows the problem and the red arrow is the wrinkle:

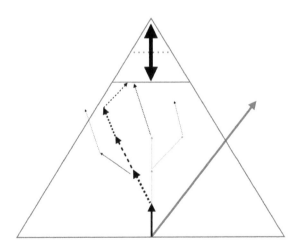

The red arrow is a whistleblower and it is worth pausing to reflect on whistleblowers. Because whistleblowing is a sign of a culture that buries bad news NEDs must be alert to this. Put another way, why is the friction above the whistleblower so great that in desperation they go to the top of the organisation or even outside with their story?

There are two important reasons NEDs should take whistle-blowing seriously:

1. It is an indicator of the health of the organisation's culture
2. Whistleblowers need and deserve protection

On the first point, it can be difficult to work out whether whistleblowing is pointing to a good or a bad culture.

Let us consider zero whistleblowing in an organisation. If staff feel able to speak up safely you are unlikely to get any whistleblowing. This is because it is OK to tell the boss the ugly truth. So, is whistleblowing a canary in the mine, zero whistle-blowers equals good culture? Well no, not always.

A lack of whistleblowers can also be because the whistle-blowing hotline is on the Deputy CEO's desk. A great friend of the CEO. Surely, that would never happen. Sorry, yes it did and the NEDs in that firm were immensely proud they had no whistleblowers.

Speaking up safely does not happen by osmosis and we have seen how drivers of behaviour can be malign. What if the drivers are for income at all costs under a CEO who brooks no dissent? Well my bet is few will feel able to speak up safely.

While I support speaking up do bear in mind that "speak up" sounds like a command. Speak up, or else what? Speak up sounds like it is the responsibility of the workforce. To turn the responsibility round add safely. Speak up safely. Now you have landed the responsibility where it belongs, the board.

Speaking up safely is not only about encouragement. It's also about instilling a culture where not being able to speak up safely would be odd. We are back to aligning drivers of behaviour with the behaviours we need to deliver our purpose. And so from junior management to senior leaders everyone values and acts on feedback.

You know there is a problem when the concerns expressed in workforce focus groups are as follows:

- It is often management who try to stop the workforce from bringing up issues
- Whistleblowers are trouble makers
- There is no protection against retaliation
- No-one trusts confidentiality or that there will be effective follow-up of reported issues

Now consider if the focus groups produced this feedback instead:

- Managers encourage and celebrate feedback. Negative feedback is a valuable means to improve the business
- Retaliation is unheard of
- There is total trust that confidentiality will be observed when asked for. And issues will be followed up and where possible rectified

Part of getting this to work is having a well thought out whistleblowing process. You can't avoid this. You can't work on the basis that your culture is so great everyone will feel able to speak up safely. The inquiry into Mid Staffs hospital found this when a nurse described her experience:

*I was concerned about the terrible effect that our actions were having on patient care. I did raise this with Sisters [X] and [Y], however their response was extremely aggressive, basically telling me that they were in charge and accusing me and anyone else who agreed with me of not being team players.*[1]

Start off by making clear the distinction between anonymity and confidentiality. Both must be assured. It is especially important that the organisation will not try to identify those who report anonymously.

The next step is to be clear that any form of retaliation, or any attempt to compromise anonymity, will be severely dealt with. Speaking up safely means the word safely has to be acted upon.

At the same time it is important to be clear that abusive or false whistleblowing will be also be dealt with. There has to be two way responsibility. The firm will protect the whistleblower from retaliation. But by the same token, the whistleblower has to act in good faith and not for instance maliciously settle personal scores.

The foundation of any whistleblowing policy is that the burden of proof is on the organisation. If there is an accusation of retaliation the burden is on management to rebut this. They must show that the same action would be taken against the whistle-blower in the absence of the whistleblowers report.

It is important to repeat that confidentiality has primacy. Which means that disclosure of a whistleblower's identity may lead to disciplinary proceedings.

Finally, be clear that the whistleblower is not Sherlock Holmes. They have no responsibility for proving or investigating what they allege. And, if a concern made in good faith proves unfounded the whistleblower must still be protected from retaliation.

It is human nature not to complain to your boss and to put a gloss on things for consumption up the line. Rocking the boat is not seen as a good career move. Getting critical comment requires constant encouragement. Another key leadership activity is to talk to intermediaries in whom your workforce might confide. An important example is a trade or staff union.

The epic miss-selling by UK banks of Personal Protection Insurance (PPI) is an example of where the warnings of the workforce to their unions went unheard at the top of banks. The workforce knew the problem, the unions were told, but there was no way for the unions to be heard by the board. People will often tell their union representative what they will not tell their manager.

The Parliamentary Commission heard this from the Unite Union:

> *Clearly, there was growing discomfort among our members that perhaps the products they were selling were not all they were cracked up to be".*[2]

My experience is that a good relationship with unions provides a source of high quality feedback from front line staff. The proof was in the pudding. Through meetings with Union leaders I learned of concerns and dissatisfaction which staff had not been able to tell management.

There is of course a challenge here "how can the culture be so bad that people won't express concerns to management?" Well, some people will feel able to express concerns to management, others won't, but to ignore that the union has information that is in all interests to share is immature. Imagine management incentives are to hit big profit targets, which may lead to poor practices. Which poor practices staff cannot tell their manager about because their manager is complicit.

Getting to a point where burying bad news does not happen is a long and hard journey. It means NEDs must have quality feedback from diverse sources including from outside the chain of command. After all it may be the chain of command that is the problem. It also means that criticism is an opportunity to learn and improve, not a chance to wield a big stick. Whistleblowing conveys a broader cultural message than the case about which the whistle has been blown.

Remember the bellwether: *"boss, we have a problem, the ugly truth is ..."*

So far we have discussed the barriers and filters that impede communication. Another impediment is peer pressure. The diagram below is of the chain of command in any large organisation. There may be several layers of middle management but at the end of the day these are the key links in the chain.

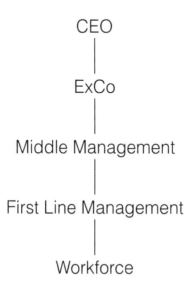

CEO

ExCo

Middle Management

First Line Management

Workforce

Peer pressure is exerted at all points of this chain of command and can easily overcome the effectiveness of upwards communication.

Take the First Line Managers who are key opinion formers in the workforce and so have an important impact on culture. Let us say there are a group of eight First Line Managers reporting into a Middle Manager. Due to natural rotation a new First Line Manager is appointed to fill a vacancy. After a month or so the new manager has found out that her team are taking short cuts and overall not doing a quality job. The Manager talks to some of the more experienced of her peers and is told: 'we all have to work with this' ... 'the systems are too poor to do the job properly' ... 'just do your best and keep a lid on it'. The first line manager, troubled by this, in the end discusses it with her boss the Middle Manager and gets the same message, 'keep a lid on it'.

Now let us take our tale up the hierarchy to the CEO. Perhaps the CEO has spotted a general quality problem reported to the board in the complaint numbers. The CEO announces to the board the formation of a new team of fifteen people to investigate and get on top of the problem. After the board meeting the Finance Director takes the CEO to one side and reminds her that there is no budget for fifteen expensive people. Also, that there is an analysts meeting shortly where the analysts already know the dividend is under pressure. The Finance Director also talks about this to a NED he knows well and before long all of the NEDs and the Chair are in active discussion. The result is a private word from the Chair to the CEO and the project team idea is quietly dropped.

The result of all this is that poor quality and customer complaints continue. First line teams and managers hear the exhortations about great service. But, having to deliver a service below what the organisation claims, will lose trust in senior management.

The tale here is of the difficulty of communication. Both the CEO and new First Line Manager are trying to do the right thing. Both are being dissuaded by peer pressure. Additionally, if the new First Line Manager does blow the whistle all the way up to the CEO will this galvanise action?

The tale is also of a Purpose that is adrift from the drivers of behaviour. The resulting culture is one of keeping your head down and toeing the party line, no matter how ugly the truth might be.

1. The Mid Staffordshire NHS Foundation Trust Public Inquiry—Chaired by Robert Francis QC—Vol 1 page 108—February 2013
2. House of Lords House of Commons
    Changing banking for good Report of the Parliamentary Commission on Banking Standards

# 28

## IT'S OK TO BE DIFFERENT

P eople approach problems in different ways. Understanding this is key to effective corporate communication.

One way to explain this is the Myers Briggs Type Indicator (MBTI). Its extra benefit is in helping to explain how communication passes throughout the firm.

MBTI is far from the only tool available to Boards. My discussing it here is to understand why analysis of this kind is important rather than that MBTI should be the toolkit of choice.

There are four MBTI constructs as shown below[1].

| E | Extroversion | ← → | Introversion | I |
|---|---|---|---|---|
| S | Sensing | ← → | iNtuition | N |
| T | Thinking | ← → | Feeling | F |
| J | Judging | ← → | Perceiving | P |

Everybody will have a preferred position on the construct, with emphasis on 'preferred'. The letters in circles are shorthand. They show a persons preference: e.g., ENTJ, is of someone with a preference for Extraversion, iNtuition, Thinking and Judging.

Our preference is analogous to writing with our preferred hand. A left handed person can write with their right hand but it takes effort, and thought. Without a lot of practice it is not as polished as writing left handedly. In the same way a preference for extraversion does not mean one cannot adopt an introversion approach, it just takes more effort.

The figure below expands the four preferences, albeit still in short-hand.

| | | |
|---|---|---|
| Extraversion...often like to bounce ideas off others and talk it out | I'm Energised... | Introversion...find they work best if they can build in plenty of quiet time to think it through |
| Sensing...find they trust and pay attention to specifics | I Pay Attention to... | iNtuition...find they look for and need the big picture |
| Thinking...often base their decisions on logical implications | I Base My Decisions on... | Feeling...often base their decisions on the Impact on people |
| Judging...often like to wrap it up | My Preferred Lifestyle is... | Perceiving...usually make no decision before it's time |

The key theme is valuing differences as opposed to looking for right and wrong. The potential for conflict between people with opposing approaches is manifold. As an example take two people, one with a preference for Judging and one for Perceiving. They are likely to find each others different approach to decision making difficult. The "J" will want to close down, make the decision, move on. The "P" will not want to make the decision until all the information needed or available is collected and understood.

In its worst manifestation a "P" looks like a hopeless procrastinator to a "J". And to a "P", well a "J" may look trigger happy and prone to jump to conclusions. Its best manifestation is when both see their strengths as helping them make better joint decisions.

This type of analysis, whether via MBTI or some other tool, is a very good way of improving communications in a group. This is particularly so in a small group such as a Board.

Important though this is there is also great value in understanding the impact throughout the whole organisation. Research done at Ashridge Management School throws up interesting dynamics for large organisations.

> ... ...*NT's are the group most likely to self select into management, and SF's are the group most likely to self-select out of management.*[2]

The table below shows us the challenge.

| NT Management | SF Workforce |
| --- | --- |
| iNtuition...find they look for and need the big picture | Feeling...often base their decisions on the impact on people |
| Thinking...often base their decisions on logical implications | Sensing...find they trust and pay attention to specifics |

We can portray the impact of this within an organisation as shown below. The NT management express their preferred view at the top of the organisation but the work force express a different preference.

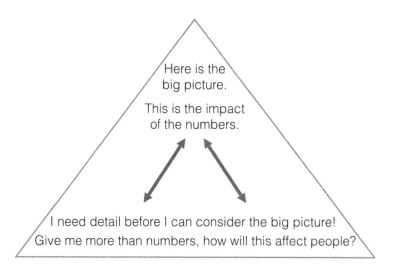

The implication is for communication. We have discussed the impact of friction when communicating up, down and through a large organisation. We now have to add to the problem of friction the impact of language. If the management craft the message in what we might call "NT-speak" this will have little or no resonance with most of the workforce who have "SF-ears".

Explaining the importance of market share to an "SF" work force won't work well. This is not because the front line are unintelligent, lazy or disinterested. But, that market share sounds both logical and big picture. Explaining the positive impact the products will have on customers is a better key to unlocking performance.

The negative impact of getting this wrong is of course immense. The "NT" management who explain the excellence of the product to a values based "SF" workforce who know the product to be a complete dog are playing with fire.

A striking example I know of happened in a branch based retail bank. Senior management had worked out that much of the savings balances sat in one account. This made it almost impossible to change the price as the impact on profit was immense. A winning scheme was developed comprising a new range of savings accounts, but these accounts would not be available to existing customers. This enabled management to degrade the rate on the original account and offer great rates on the new account to new customers with much less impact on profit than if the great rate was offered on the original account. Very logical, very big picture, but very unfair (to existing loyal customers).

The branch based staff effectively rebelled against this perceived 'unfairness'. Loyal to their customers they helped them find ways around this. They would close the old account and then re-open a new account, even to the extent of registering the person as a new customer. Head office issued strident edicts but all this did was drive the activity underground. Staff were even dealing with customers at home and in the evening. Eventually the restriction had to be lifted, but it took months of ill feeling. Staff remembered this for years afterwards, long after the NT management responsible for the winning scheme had left.

This whole discussion about MBTI has been by way of example. The intention is to highlight not only the way different people come to decisions, but also that the way these decisions are broadcast may well be different to the way they are received.

The impact around the board room is two-fold.

Firstly, if not understood then differences can lead to discord but further than that wise counsel may go unremarked. It is especially the case that introverts (the "I" in MBTI type terms) may not be heard. A top tip for Chairs is to listen hard for the people who don't say much, because when they do speak what they have to say tends to be important. Without meaning to the expressive extraverts are well able to drown out the thoughtful quiet voices of introvert colleagues. Judgements are better when they come through the fire of challenge and that means hearing everyone on the board.

Secondly, NEDs will want to know that these dynamics are

thought about by the executives when designing important communications to the whole organisation.

In summary, whilst far from easy, quality communication is hugely important and it is front and centre part of the NED's assurance role.

Communication is even more important in a period of change during which the support and wise counsel of NEDs is at a premium. Therefore, it is worth looking at change next.

1. The MBTI was constructed by Katharine Cook Briggs and her daughter Isabel Briggs Myers. It is based on the conceptual theory proposed by Carl Jung.
2. Ashridge Management School MBTI Research into distribution of type— Carr, Curd and Dent.

# 29

# THE DARK NIGHT OF THE INNOVATOR

This final word about communication is to do with change. The figure below shows a typical change curve and my favourite description of the worst point on the curve: the dark night of the innovator.

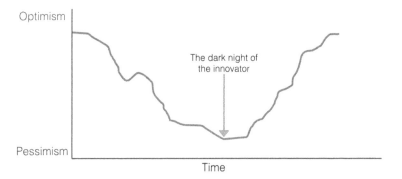

One problem for the leader is that in communicating a change to others the 'others' will experience their own change curve. But, this will start later than the leader's and some of the 'others' will be more optimistic and some less so. The result is an overlay of change curves which as shown below do not coincide at all with the leader's.

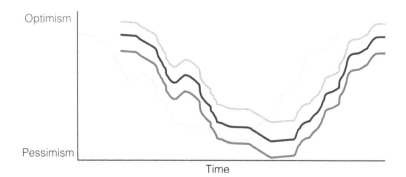

This is further complicated because some people deal with change very quickly whilst for others the implications dawn much more slowly. Which adds two different shaped curves to our diagram as shown below.

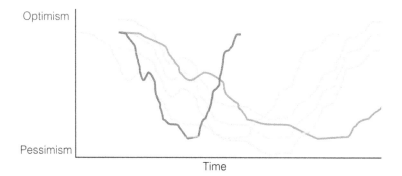

Simplifying for the final diagram you can see the leader's change curve just does not get anywhere close to coinciding with others change curves for the reasons of both personal outlook and timing.

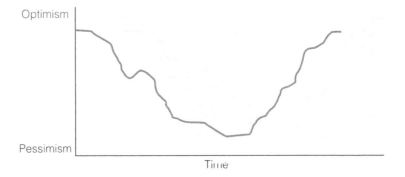

Let me also use this typology to touch on the personal stress that change brings. It is no good the leader of the change telling everyone how under pressure they are feeling because one of the roles of the leader is to give followers hope on the journey. Part of the leader's stress of course is in being seen to be optimistic whilst from time to time feeling pessimistic. The gap between the optimism line, dotted in the figure below, which may be what the leader needs to communicate, and how they are actually feeling is one measure of stress along the way.

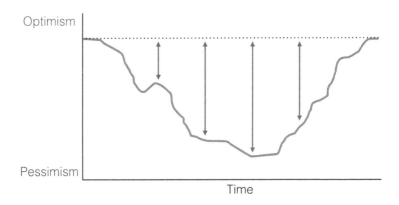

Figuratively, the amount of stress shown by the red arrows argues leaders need two supporting change mechanisms: the first is good research and planning. The less research and planning there is the more risk the change will be unsuccessful and the more pressure there is on the leader. The second is the need for wise supportive counsel and critical friendship. This is front and centre the role of the Chair and NEDs especially as far as a CEO is concerned.

There is a risk here, and that is to the first behavioural driver, trustworthiness. It is too easy to step over a line of being optimistic about the way forward to being dishonest about it. People will respond to a challenge, but eventually they will see through an argument that glosses over the truth. The ugly truth is sometimes not what anyone wants to hear but it is often what they need to hear.

Communicating an 'all is well' message when there is no thought through plan to get over the change finish line is a betrayal of trust. Any course charted by the CEO and board must be grounded on good research and planning not a forlorn hope.

The moral of change is to communicate and to keep communicating, this is as important as preparation and a good plan.

*However, even in those departments anticipating considerable downsizing, people responded more positively on all of these dimensions when they felt that their own management was trustworthy, communicated honestly with them, and listened to their concerns.*[1]

I'll finish this chapter on communication with a quote from Sir Peter Hendy the CEO of Transport for London who went on to lead the organisation of the London Olympic Games in 2012. This is not a depressing fact but a helpful warning:

*However much you tell people somebody hasn't listened.*

1. Motivating Creativity in Organisations: On Doing What You Love And Loving What You Do—Teresa M. Amabile

# 30

# DECISION MAKING

The third driver of behaviour is decision making, not obvious but nonetheless powerful. It's key part in culture is revealed in the HIH Insurance inquiry:

> *By 'corporate culture' I mean the charism or personality— sometimes overt but often unstated—that guides the decision-making process at all levels of an organisation. In the case of HIH, the culture that developed was inimical to sound management practices. It resulted in decision making that fell well short of the required standards.*[1]

The first point to grasp about decision making is that the board and senior management will be subject to 'boss watching' by people throughout the organisation. Not only will judgement be passed on what decisions are made but also how the fallout from great and poor decisions is handled, the decisions that over time are proven to be cup winners or awful mistakes.

The way decisions are made is a major signpost of culture for the organisation and to unpick decision making I offer three dimensions: *logic*, *manner* and *mandate*.

Considering *logic* as a dimension simply reflects the Nobel prize winning work of Daniel Kahneman[2] whose research points to two ways in which we all reach decisions:

> *System 1 operates automatically and quickly, with little or no effort and no sense of voluntary control ...*
>
> *System 2 allocates attention to the effortful mental activities that demand it, including complex computations. The operations of System 2 are often associated with the subjective experience of agency, choice, and concentration ...*

I cannot possibly do Kahneman's work proper justice and if you wish to understand better I recommend you read his book, *Thinking Fast and Slow*[3]. However, I will say that executive behaviour in coming to judgements shows to what extent decisions are system 1 or system 2.

If there is a good regime of researched and thoughtful papers produced ahead of board meetings that give Executive and Non-Executive Directors time to consider aspects of key decisions then System 2 is in play. However, if papers are late, poorly written or non-existent then the organisation is relying on System 1, the gut feel of people who in very little time agree on a way forward.

System 1 is also a feature of a weak Chair who, not supporting challenge from NEDs, allows decision making by the CEO and executives to happen outside the board room. Another example from the failure of HIH illustrates the problem.

> *The board was heavily dependent on the advice of senior management: there were very few occasions when the board either rejected or materially changed a proposal put forward by management.*[4]

Decision making is a key part of tone from the top and it will permeate an organisation. The board who react at short notice to events, with little good thinking written down for consideration, is guaranteed to have an organisation below it that does exactly the same.

One of the difficult lessons of life is to learn how not to make decisions in haste, except when demanded by the most difficult of crisis situations. It is also important that skilful drafting of well researched papers is not seen as some arcane Dickensian skill left over from gentler times. Good papers prepare a board for good discussions. This ensures the big and important decisions not only pass through the fire of challenge but are insulated from reactive 'gut feel'.

'Gut feel' is especially dangerous in the presence of a dominant CEO or Chair for whom the phrase 'brooks no dissent' fits like a latex glove. Which thought takes us to the second decision making dimension, *manner*.

CEOs are likely to be dominant characters, however, it is how that dominance manifests itself that makes the difference. Collaborative and collegiate may in some quarters be read as signs of weakness, but if the collegiality and collaboration leads to better decisions that improve the business then that is one form of dominance for the good. Again HIH Insurance helps illustrate the problem:

> *The CEO was, in reality, chief executive from the inception of the business until he stepped aside in October 2000. No one rivalled him in terms of authority or influence. Even as his business judgment faltered in the second half of the 1990s he remained unchallenged.*[5]

To help you visualise what I mean consider a scale of Collaborative through to Authoritative as follows:

You will see the brake on the CEO's manner is the way the NEDs interact. When you think about it this is exactly so. The CEO can only inflict unfortunate habits on the organisation if the NEDs allow it. If the CEO is a dominant character then challenge is very likely to be suppressed and this lack of challenge becomes the way we do things around here. The tough call for NEDs is when this sort of CEO is realising excellent financial results. Do the NEDs support a culture of results at any cost or deal with the bad behaviour and call the CEO to account. This is a defining moment for a board.

The arrow heads are not casually drawn. On the left the NEDs may have to constantly draw the CEO in this direction, pulling to the left. The pace of the CEOs life, the complexity of decisions and the constant management of the next issue will all tend to drive the CEO towards the right hand of the scale.

On the right hand side the arrow shows the push of the dominant CEO to establish a strong and unassailable position. Any challenge being either suppressed or weak by design: for instance the CEO influencing the recruitment of NEDs to make it so. We have discussed the importance of the Chair of the board already but now the real impact of the weak Chair is apparent.

The third and final decision making dimension is *mandate*.

Mandate might sound bureaucratic and frankly it is. Unfortunately, bureaucrat and bureaucratic come with all sorts of negative connotations. However, having clarity around who takes decisions is at the heart of good decision making. Lack of clarity around mandates will lead to decisions being made all over the organisation by the strongest characters, who may well not be the best decision makers. Nor, even worse, have the experience and expertise needed to make the right judgements that lead to the right final decision.

The opposition to this will come from those who disbelieve the value of organising: those who believe that in this modern world of rapidly advancing technology bureaucracy has to be shaken off. This nonsense has to be resisted, great leaders are clear about the responsibilities of their followers, this especially applies to who can take which decisions.

These three dimensions of decision making: logic, manner and mandate, are leadership dimensions. They help measure in which way decisions are made at board and executive level and are of course behaviours that set examples and models for the whole organisation to follow.

Leading this senior behaviour is the Chair who has the power to enhance or fatally wound good, well challenged, board decision making. A crucial point on this was made by Sir Adrian Cadbury, getting broad agreement is not the same as getting to a good decision:

> ... *the Chair's job is to see the board reaches not merely a consensus but a good decision.*[6]

There is a mirror to this senior behaviour and that is the workforce's memory of how decisions have been made in the past.

The workforce's experience of past decision-making guides current and future decisions. For example, a firm with a historically strong low cost ethic will be making low cost decisions at levels throughout the firm. If the firm is successful in its industry because of its low cost approach to business then low cost decisions will be celebrated. Now imagine the challenge of a change of strategy that moves away from low cost, let us say to innovation, requiring a high and continual investment in R&D.

This is why change is so difficult. Change means new decisions have to fly in the face of how decisions were made in the past and what is perceived to be 'the way we do things around here'. In short, behaviours have to change. That which has previously guided the organisation on a day to day basis is suddenly in disarray, the guide has been lost.

Understanding this explains the complexity of culture change. The new culture, in the form of a new framework for making decisions which means behaving differently, has to be explained. "Why are we doing things differently?", and "what is it I have to do differently?" These are key questions senior management have to communicate repeatedly.

Of course, no matter how well this is done, if the other behavioural drivers in *Stage 2* remain unchanged old habits will die very hard.

The next part of decision making is to understand that some decisions have results that cannot be quickly measured. This is called the time span of discretion.

1. HIH Royal Commission. The failure of HIH Insurance—ISBN 0 9750678 5 0 (set)—April 2003
2. Thinking, Fast and Slow by Daniel Kahneman
3. Ibid.
4. HIH Royal Commission. The failure of HIH Insurance—ISBN 0 9750678 5 0 (set)—April 2003
5. Ibid.
6. Corporate Governance and Chairship: A Personal View—Adrian Cadbury

# 31

# TIME SPAN OF DISCRETION

I n the 1980s hierarchy was being challenged and only one management thinker, Eliot Jaques, appears to have defended it. The reason I am zeroing in on hierarchy is that a set of mandates is by definition hierarchical. Jaques point on hierarchy is that this is the way the human race organises itself naturally in family groups, and he questioned the drive for flatter structures which in the 1980's was just gathering pace. I too have this problem with the 'removal of hierarchy' crowd, fine I think, but what instead?

At the centre of hierarchy is judgement and decision making and this comes, according to Jaques, with a time span:

> *Any task has both a **what** to be accomplished and a **by-when**.....the **by-when** is the longest maximum-target-completion-time set by the manager for that particular output.....the longest of the maximum-target-completion-times of tasks in the role gives a direct measure of the level of work of the role.*[1]

Jaques called this *direct measure* the *Time-Span of Discretion*.

Compare the judgement made by a cashier who accepts, without counting, a bundle of £50 notes to a CEO who gets board approval for a hostile acquisition where limited due diligence is possible. At the end of the day (literally) the cashier's till will balance or not. The 'end of the day' balancing of the acquisition led by the CEO may not be for five or more years.

Five to seven years is a typical time-span of discretion for the few judgements at organisational level the Board, both NEDs and Executives, make. The determination of strategy is not going to result in quick proof one way or the other as regards the quality of the judgement made. The notion that quick, lightly considered decisions should be made when the outturn may not be proven for years is exposed.

The few fundamental decisions boards should be making are going to include those long time-span judgements. Consequently these should not be allocated a trivial amount of the board's time. Strategy is a major judgement the board needs to get right. Equally, getting the right culture in place to fully support the board's effective oversight of risk is not an overnight activity, nor is the outcome going to be clear within a few months.

This takes us back to the mandates point. Decision making mandates should reflect the seniority of the person. In other words don't hand out a mandate for decisions with a time span of discretion of four years to a first level manager: Jaques estimated the time span of discretion for first line managers to be about three months. Three months relating to these managers main influence which is recruitment and process.

There are three reasons for getting mandates right. First, and I hope obviously, you want the right level of experience and seniority attaching to the right level of decision. If your decision making responsibility is above a person's ability you are not only likely to wind up with poor decisions but also a lot of stress for the person involved. The reverse, in which a person with ability is only allowed to make trivial decisions creates a different kind of stress but no better decisions. This is because the decisions have been sucked up a level and are occupying the time of someone who should be spending time on bigger decisions. This is the classic micro management problem.

The induction challenge for the newly promoted manager is coaching in the higher level decision making they should be expected to achieve. This means oversight by the next level up to help coach and develop this ability.

When corporate governance is reviewed there is often a piece of file checking, has the board delegated powers in an appropriate way to its sub committees and executives. However, as important is how does the CEO and ExCo delegate decision making, is this structured and clear or is it assumed and opaque?

One of the biggest lessons to learn about judgement is the need for challenge. This is something that the organisation should bake into its mandate policy. A mandate does not make you the sole arbiter of the decision, it means you are the person to make the final call on what the decision is after taking soundings from others and listening to opposing views. Peter Drucker was clear on the need for challenge and its impact on good judgement when he wrote:

> *Effective executives, finally make effective decisions. They know that this is, above all, a matter of system—of the right steps in the right sequence. They know that an effective decision is always a judgement based on "dissenting opinions" rather than a "consensus of the facts." And they know that to make many decisions fast means to make the wrong decisions. What is needed are few, but fundamental, decisions. What is needed is the right strategy rather than razzle dazzle tactics*[2].

Drucker not only draws our attention to the need for

*dissenting opinions* but also to the *few, but fundamental, deci-sions.* These few but fundamental decisions are what should pre-occupy the time of boards, and good Chairs are the ones that can set aside and protect the time and energy needed to focus on these. The trap to fall into is that of process overcoming outcomes. The few fundamental decisions boards should be focusing on are those to do with strategy, business model viability and sustainability, recruitment and retention of talent, culture and risk oversight. An audit of how the board spends its time may well find the total given over to these subjects is less than 50%, it may be a lot less.

The self awareness of boards that they must focus on 'the few fundamental decisions' is a highly valuable first step, the check that it does so an important second step and the adjustment of focus if it finds itself in the weeds of process and/or small decisions an essential third step.

One of the Board's few fundamental decisions surely is that it checks it is focusing its own time correctly. Returning to Drucker, he makes this point through a whole chapter devoted to 'Know Thy Time':

> *'Know thyself' the old prescription for wisdom, is almost impossibly difficult for mortal men. But everyone can follow the injunction 'Know Thy Time'.....and be well on the road toward contribution and effectiveness*[3].

Judgement is exercised every day at all levels from 'how many graduates should we recruit next year' up to 'should we acquire that business?'. There are great individual challenges to making good judgements, not least of which is recognising and allowing for any personal bias. Kahneman is again an excellent source of reference about these dangers, providing a useful tip which is particularly applicable to board discussions, a tip that can obviously only be deployed under good leadership by the board Chair:

> *A simple rule can help: before an issue is discussed, all members of the committee should be asked to write a very brief summary of their position. This procedure makes good use of the value of the diversity of knowledge and opinion in the group. The standard practice of open discussion gives too much weight to the opinions of those who speak early and assertively, causing others to line up behind them*[4].

Boards are unlikely to be full of shrinking violets and so Kahneman's advice about guarding against the early and assertive speakers is sound. You will also appreciate the space this gives to the Myers Briggs *Introverts*.

Summarising this section on judgement: in my view this is the one competence boards cannot do without. Making bad judgements will in the end lead to perdition, from taxpayers bailing out a failed bank to dreadful standards of care in a hospital. My argument is that everything a board does about its composition, diversity, time together and working relationships must always lead to continually honing, sharpening and improving the board's ability to make good decisions.

In summary then, the key to good decision making is across three dimensions: *logic*, *manner* and *mandate* as shown below.

Are decisions thought through or gut feel/off the cuff?

Are decisions made through the fire of constructive challenge?

Is it clear at what level decisions can be made?

Remember the notion of the few, but fundamental decisions. In Jaques terms these will be the decisions with the long time-span of discretion: such as the strategy, the core system replacement, the risk appetite. These are the matters that should occupy the time of the executive and board.

Finally, recognition that all decisions will have some degree of unpopularity is summed up beautifully by a Paratrooper writing of his experience leading a company in combat. His words apply to everyone, including NEDs, in a timeless way:

*I find myself returning to my mantra over and over again, 'The popular decision will be right some of the time: the right decision will be right all of the time'.*[5]

1. Requisite Organisation—Elliott Jaques 1988
2. The Effective Executive: The Definitive Guide to Getting the Right Things Done - Peter F Drucker - 1967
3. Ibid.
4. Thinking, Fast and Slow by Daniel Kahneman
5. Lewis, Russell. Company Commander (p. 403). Ebury Publishing. Kindle Edition. ISBN: 9780753540305

# 32

# DRUCKER, EISENHOWER AND TIME MANAGEMENT

Yes, I know, time management. Right up there with risk management as a reason for a reader to put a book down in favour of any other activity.

However, from a board perspective it is worth a look.

My search led me to realise I needed a framework rather than a tool. The solution in the end surprised me. I found it by merging the work of Peter Drucker[1] with a speech President Eisenhower made in 1954. This is the key excerpt from the speech:

> *"I illustrate it by quoting the statement of a former college president ... This president said, "I have two kinds of problems, the urgent and the important. The urgent are not important, and the important are never urgent."*[2]

Drucker laid great store in measuring how time has been spent on activities in the past. He exhorted executives to *know thy time*[3]. And he pointed out that it is good practice to measure manual work through time and motion. Strangely this is not so for management and boards. It is a telling indictment that

Drucker wrote about this in 1967 and yet here we are 50 years later, still wrestling with the subject.

The merger of Drucker and Eisenhower is through a four box matrix some call the Eisenhower model.

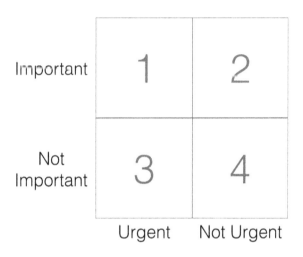

Start unpacking this by thinking about your own time.

In box 1 you get the action that DEMANDS your time NOW. Those last minute crises. The forgotten item on your non-existent to do list. The presentation for the conference you agreed to six months ago that is due tomorrow.

In box 2 are activities that sit in the background. They are every bit as important as box 1, but don't shout at you. Time with your family, thinking and planning time, going to the gym. All the stuff you wish you'd done after the moment has passed.

Box 3 is urgent but it's not important. It's the e-mails that you keep fiddling back to all day. The drop-in visitor who consumes 30 minutes but contributes little to your important objectives.

Box 4 is a waste of time, some meetings are here, simply wasted time.

The extension of this to the time boards spend together

provides a similar analysis. 'Important' now refers to the contribution to and development of the firm's *Purpose*. The board agenda and sub-committee agendas act as proxies for how the board spends its time. Any secretariat should be able to help a board get to grips with its prioritisation of time as shown below:

|  | 1 | 2 |
|---|---|---|
| Important | Crises of some sort or another leading to unplanned activity | Purpose Strategy Risk Framework |
|  | 3 | 4 |
| Not Important | e.g. Governance and compliance requirements | Matters the board should not be spending time on |
|  | Urgent | Not Urgent |

The key is to get directors thinking about how the board spends its time. Having some form of framework is not unhelpful. The contents of the boxes are of course open to debate but here are my thoughts on each:

Box 1—crises will always happen and have to be dealt with by the board. The sudden unplanned departure of a key executive. The unexpected bid from a competitor or activist investor. The collapse of a key market, unforeseen financial loss or the loss of a profitable contract. The question is not how to stop this kind of external matter falling into box 1. But rather to curtail what might be termed self-inflicted box 1 activity. To what extent has the board itself contributed to a 'box 1 crisis'? Examples such as poor operational resilience plans. Late production of the report and accounts. Notice of an important strategic debate given at such short notice that several directors can't make it. These sort of events should always be the subject of scrutiny.

Equally, many of these 'unexpected events' can be planned for. In the event of a surprise bid for the business what is the game plan? If our system defences are breached what is the game plan? This is basic risk management which is often reserved for IT systems. Yet, operational resilience should be broad and cover the whole business. The game plans must go beyond the IT systems to include such as the unwelcome bid or emergency succession planning.

Assembling and practising these game plans is of course box two activity.

Box 2—The central point to Box 2 is the all important *Purpose* of the firm which we talked of earlier. Development of strategy and risk management. These are two examples of key decisions that need the time and energy of the board. But, because they are not crises, they may not attract the board's attention. In the end though a badly thought through and badly executed Risk Appetite will attract the board's attention. Risks which have been inadequately identified, measured and miti-gated will crystallise and appear in Box 1 as crises. Equally, a flawed strategy may not be immediately clear. But, in the end, its impact may produce such a crisis as to ruin the organisation, never mind missing its *Purpose*.

Box 3—I am not saying that governance and compliance requirements are unimportant. I am saying that they are not important to the core *Purpose* of the firm. These are the neces-sary administrative backdrop to the board's business as usual. Great governance and compliance ought to be a matter of course and support Box 2 activity. They should not, as is too often the case, crowd out value added box 2 activity.

Box 4—The board agenda I saw with the staff canteen prices as the second item falls into this category. I might add the agenda item about the debenture box at Lords but enough is probably enough in making the point.

The Chair and an able secretariat can easily track the way the board spends its time. It may or may not use a framework such as the Drucker/Eisenhower hybrid. However, the essential information for the Chair is how the board has spent its time. And also, and most instructively, what the forward board agenda looks like. How is the board intending to spend its time?

I also looked at board time management through the lens of failing organisations. I found in the HIH inquiry the Chair leaving the board agenda in the hands of the CEO. This is an extreme example of the executive driving the board but it is an important point to make. The agenda drives what the board will spend time on. It is crucial the Chair and NEDs own it.

I will now turn to the impact of regulation, represented by box 3. A perennial complaint of boards is that regulation drowns out important activity. For instance strategy discussions in box 2. Take as an example the Dodd-Frank Wall Street Reform and Consumer Protection Act. Even the name is a mouthful. This is the major regulatory response in the USA to the 2008 crisis. It now runs to the equivalent of 28 copies of Tolstoy's War and Peace[4].

The danger is that regulation defines what the board does. For example: 'this board has independent NEDs because the regulator says we must'. This completely misses the point. The reason the regulator wants independent NEDs ought to be the same reason the organisation wants independent NEDs. Independent NEDs provide independent challenge, the clue is in the name. By definition this ought to result in better quality judgements.

This all leads to an interesting line of thought. Why has regulation been increasing over very many years? Consider the three lines of defence model often adopted by organisations:

Line 1—the business managing its own risks

Line 2—the risk function, guardian of the Risk Appetite Framework. Ensuring Line 1 adheres to it

Line 3—internal audit, giving assurance to the board over the financial numbers, financial controls and the activities of Lines 1 and 2

Defining the three lines in a different way begs a question. Is the increasing volume of rules caused by a systemic failure of non executives? What if the three lines look like this instead:

Line 1—the executives

Line 2—the non-executives

Line 3—the regulator

If non-executives fail to hold executives to account then it is all down to the regulator. In which case don't be surprised at the tempo and volume of regulatory rule-making.

What if a magic wand removed all regulation? How then are hospital care standards and consumer protection assured? Who prevents taxpayers having to bale out banks? In this thought experiment you can see the case for strong and thoughtful NED wisdom.

NEDs have to deliver a complex agenda and it is not possible to do this in a vacuum of expectations. Drucker wrote about the effective executive. I mentally adjust his meaning to include the effective non-executive. Effective non-executives should appraise the time the board is spending on different activities. Inevitably there will be slippage into the weeds of boxes 3 and 4. Too many energy sapping crises in box 1. In these circumstances it is the NEDs who must pull the board back into box 2.

A major box 2 activity is the annual review of strategy and corporate planning. As a final component of decision making that is where we go next.

1. The Effective Executive : The Definitive Guide to Getting the Right Things Done—Peter Drucker
2. President Dwight D. Eisenhower: "Address at the Second Assembly of the World Council of Churches, Evanston, Illinois.," August 19, 1954.
3. The Effective Executive : The Definitive Guide to Getting the Right Things Done—Peter Drucker
4. Research by Davis Polk—July 2013—3 Years of Dodd Frank—davis-polk.com

# 33

# SETTING STRATEGY

O ne major decision boards make every year is to review and where necessary reset the firm's strategy. I'm not going to get into a debate about whether an annual review is the right way to approach setting strategy. I simply note this is what most firms do and so it exists as a good example of a key decision.

Now ... remember the words of the Higgs report:

*Non-executive directors should constructively challenge and contribute to the development of strategy*[1].

This could not be clearer. But, the means by which NEDs challenge and contribute to strategy is less clear. I have met firms where 'the strategy' appears as a polished, or unpolished, document. It gets a single desultory debate and is 'signed off'. These sorts of firm also tend to be those where the NEDs do not meet as a group without the executive present. A requirement of the CEO, acquiesced to by the Chair. This is also a board where challenge is seen as divisive, or unhelpful, or not collegiate.

What about NEDs who assess 'the strategy' as poor and

recommend the CEO appoint a consultant? This may be the remedy, an external view is never a bad thing. But, it could suggest a CEO who is unable to develop strategy. This is a different NED problem to a poor proposal.

A highly regarded reference is 'Good Strategy, Bad Strategy' by Richard Rumelt[2]. Rumelt says: *Good strategy is not just "what" you are trying to do. It is also "why" and "how" you are doing it.*

I summarise NED contribution to strategy development in the four steps below.

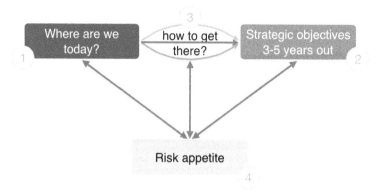

As a first step, where is the organisation today? This in itself should be a series of debates, and is of course ongoing. The next step is to be clear on where the organisation wishes to move to and why? In the diagram above this is the strategic objectives 3–5 years out. Arrival at clear strategic objectives is not achieved via a 'one-meeting-sign-this-off' approach.

The third step is how to move from step 1 to step 2. Rumelt is clear that the strategy of the firm is how to move from today. This means clarity about overcoming obstacles and thus how to achieve strategic objectives. Often this 'how to' step of a corporate plan is missing.

In the figure above I show the 'how to get there' plans as red, amber and green. There are different pathways and some will be more risky (red) than others (green and amber). A capable CEO presents options to the board for discussion and challenge. Presenting only one option suggests a CEO who does not want to engage in a debate. But rather, argue, or get rubber stamped, the single case he or she has already decided upon.

The fourth step is another dimension to this strategy debate and that is the risk appetite of the board. Literally, what appetite does the board have for taking on risk in the business? Is the start position more or less risky than the end position? What happens to risk in the intervening years, is more risk taken during the transition?

The diagram below explains the different roles played by the directors.

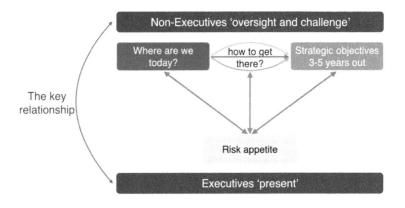

Firstly, the key relationship. This is core to how the board should operate. The non-executives request the executives to develop a strategy. They ask for this for discussion, debate and challenge at the board. They will not accept for ceremonial sign off polished, or unpolished, documents.

The inquiry into the failure of the Australian insurer HIH explains this:

*Generally speaking, it is for management, rather than the board, to propose strategy. This is not an impediment to the board taking the initiative in an appropriate case. But management is best able to dedicate time to strategic thinking and is likely to have greater industry knowledge and experience. Nevertheless, it is the board's responsibility to understand, test and endorse the company's strategy. In monitoring performance, the board needs to measure management proposals by reference to the endorsed strategy, with any deviation in practice being challenged and explained. This is what the HIH board failed to do.[3]*

There is a follow on big and difficult question for the NEDs. Having challenged and agreed the strategy how do they know the executives will follow it? Let us say the chosen strategy is a mixture of green and amber pathways with no red. After a year, the executives see they will miss their strategic objectives. With their medium term bonus at risk they may decide to shift to red. Will they tell the NEDs? If not how will the NEDS spot this? What will they do on spotting it?

In this respect inter year plans are notoriously difficult for NEDs to link together. The question is, what part does the 2012 three year plan play in the 2013 three year plan? The detailed one year plan, where years two and three contain less detail, may lead to a year 1 plan reset every year. What can be missed? Well, its the previously agreed targets. Looking at these without reset gives a consistent view of how the strategy is panning out.

Imagine a strategic objective of a cost base of £x after three years. Resetting this in year 2, which has now become the new year 1, is an excellent piece of obfuscation.

The figure below shows what happened when NEDs wised up to this three year "plan-itus". They had plotted for them, against the three year plans, what had actually been happening.

The curved lines are the three year numbers in each year's plan and the straight line the actual end year result.

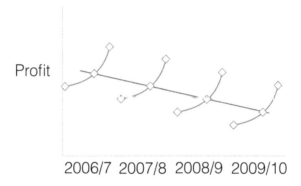

Profit

2006/7 2007/8 2008/9 2009/10

There is an old adage that the difficult challenges of the three year plan are in the fourth year. This appears to have a frightening amount of truth in it.

All of which takes us to how executive directors need to help NEDs. Andrew Bailey pointed to this when addressing the complex issue of model use in firms:

> So, let me put forward a proposition for Boards. It is the job of the Executive to be able to explain in simple and transparent terms these complex matters to Non-Executives ... In other words, they should not be pointed towards the haystack with warm wishes for the search ahead.[4]

This is very true of the corporate plan embodying as it does the whole workings of the business. Remember the key point here, the NEDs' role is to help the executives make better decisions. The quid quo pro? The executives help the NEDs by explaining, as simply as is needed, the proposed strategy and its component parts.

Rumelt advises that the strategy should not only be what you intend doing but also why and how. This reinforces Andrew

Bailey's point. The executives must explain the how and the why to enable the NEDs to challenge the plans in a constructive way.

Boards will only make a few key decisions a year. Making time for these decisions in the face of the general hurly burly is essential. As essential as time is the will of both NEDs and executives to collaborate through open debate.

We now move to incentives, which is the fourth driver of behaviour. But before we do let me close decision making with the wise words of Sir Adrian Cadbury:

> *The company's strategy and action plans may well move backwards and forwards between the board and the management until final agreement is reached on their form. The outcome is thus a board/management dialogue, rather than the board passing on a set of instructions to those who have to execute them. In this way both board and management are committed to a jointly agreed strategy.*[5]

---

1. http://www.ecgi.org/codes/documents/higgsreport.pdf
2. Good Strategy, Bad Strategy. Richard Rumelt. The Difference and Why It Matters. 2011. ISBN 978 1 84668 480 7
3. HIII Royal Commission. The failure of HIH Insurance—ISBN 0 9750678 5 0 (set)—April 2003
4. Governance and the role of Boards—Speech given by Andrew Bailey, Deputy Governor, Prudential Regulation and Chief Executive Officer, Prudential Regulation Authority—Westminster Business Forum, London 3 November 2015
5. Cadbury, Adrian. Corporate Governance and Chairship: A Personal View. OUP Oxford.

# 34

# INCENTIVES

*Whether dealing with monkeys, rats, or human beings, it is hardly controversial to state that most organisms seek information concerning what activities are rewarded, and then seek to do (or at least pretend to do) those things, often to the virtual exclusion of activities not rewarded.*[1]

T his is the introduction to the seminal paper on incentives written by Kerr in 1975. Just the title of the paper: 'On the Folly of Rewarding A, While Hoping for B' sums up one challenge of setting incentives. Writing forty years later, Muller expands on this:

*Similarly, many jobs have multiple facets, and measuring only a few aspects creates incentives to neglect the rest.*[2]

These two quotes put the incentives dilemma in a nutshell. People will tend to follow the rewards on offer but it is seldom easy to make sure those rewards cover all aspects of a job or role, or indeed contribute to delivery of the purpose of the organisation. Also, because ambiguity increases alongside role senior-ity, establishing the right measures becomes increasingly difficult the higher up the organisation you go. And, by the way, this applies to a wide range of organisations. In the past a bonus was not part of the pay package for the likes of hospital CEOs, university Vice Chancellors and charity bosses. Now it is.

When discussing model risk I noted the challenge to the credit risk modeller of finding a proxy for honesty. The same challenge exists here, what proxies should we use to measure performance?

> *For a complex job such as senior management, it is simply not possible to precisely measure someone's "actual" performance, given that it consists of many different stakeholders' interests, tangible and tacit resources, and short- and long-term effects.*[3]

Here Cable and Vermeulen talk about the CEO but this problem exists from the top to the bottom of most organisations. What are the proxies for success? In Kerr's terms what is B, and are we rewarding that or something else called A and hoping for B?

Recall the earlier story of the nurses in the Mid Staffs Accident and Emergency (A&E) unit. They were put under huge pressure to deliver A, exit patients from A&E within four hours, while hoping that the B of good quality care would be delivered. It wasn't.

As an example let's not look at a CEO but take a middle management role in a salesforce. We might identify leadership, coaching, training and quality assurance as competences sales managers need to ensure their sales people deliver good quality sales. However, these are inputs and as such are difficult to measure.

What are our sales managers measured on then? Well the clue is in the name, sales: via profit, volume and amount. These output numbers are easily measured. This risk of Rewarding A (sales volume) whilst hoping for B (good quality sales) crystallised in December 2013 when a bank was fined by the regulator for exactly this:

> *In addition, although advisers were supervised by local sales managers, the Firms failed to identify that there was a potential conflict of interest due to the fact that sales managers' bonuses were based on the performance of advisers in their teams.*[4]

Turning to the challenge a board faces in measuring the performance of the CEO. We may want our CEO to have strategic vision, leadership skills and an intuitive feel for the market.

However, rather than have the incentive scheme focus our CEO on these competences it is more usual to use a proxy such as return on equity (ROE), share price or earnings per share (EPS). The reasoning appears to be that as well as being easily measured, financial metrics align the CEO's interest with those of the shareholders. However, in Kerr's terms we reward the A of financial results and hope for the B of strategic vision, leadership skills and an intuitive feel for the market.

Ought we then to question the fixation with financial metrics? Let's find out.

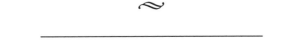

---

1. On the Folly of Rewarding A, While Hoping for B—Author(s): Steven Kerr—Source: The Academy of Management Journal, Vol. 18, No. 4 (Dec., 1975), pp. 769-783

2. Muller, Jerry Z. The Tyranny of Metrics Princeton University Press 2018 2018 ISBN 978-0-691-17495-2
3. Harvard Business Review—Stop Paying Executives for Performance by Dan Cable and Freek Vermeulen—FEBRUARY 23, 2016
4. Financial Conduct Authority—Final Notice—Lloyds TSB Bank plc Bank of Scotland plc—December 2013

# 35

# SHAREHOLDER VALUE AND PRINCIPAL AGENT

I t's a fair question to ask why senior executive bonuses are so focused on financial metrics like EPS and ROE. I referred to the principal-agent problem in the First Part and how the 1976 work on shareholder value by Jensen and Meckling has passed into corporate folklore. Their theory holds that targeting senior executives to increase shareholder value aligns their interests with the owners of the business.

In his 2012 report John Kay makes this observation about the objective of incentives:

> ... ... *the probable effect of any performance incentive is not so much to make the person or business try harder as to make them try differently.* [1]

We can see trying differently includes aligning executive interests with their principals.

At this point you may be asking what is the role of the NED as they appear to be neither principal nor agent. The answer lies in the three tier agency model. This model tackles the difficulty principals have devoting time to managing their agents.

The three tier model has the principal employing a supervisor to manage the behaviour and interests of the managers. NEDs should perform this supervision role.

Conyon and He[2] who researched the model say this:

> *Whether the supervisor will work in the principal's best interest, or instead collude with the agent, is dependent on whether the supervisor's interests are more tightly related with those of shareholders (principal) or management (agent). The value of the three-tier agency model is that it focuses attention on the supervisor's incentives to promote shareholder welfare.*

Their results are interesting:

> *Overall, our results suggest that firms with weaker governance structures have greater agency problems: that CEOs at firms with greater agency problems receive greater compensation: and that firms with greater agency problems perform worse.*[3]

The three tier agency model relies on the NEDs acting in the interest of the shareholder. Which means not colluding with the executives. But let's face it, as a NED it's a tough choice. Do you keep a low profile and your head down? Or do you take a contrary and possibly hostile stance with the executives? It is particularly the case that NEDs will not challenge if the Chair of the board does not support them. This difficult subject of NED challenge is something we will return to in a later chapter.

As ever though, nothing is as simple as it appears. An example is the sudden, dramatic collapse of Patisserie Valerie (PV). PV is an upmarket cake shop.

I'm not about to comment on the secret bank overdrafts or the discovered net debt versus the supposed net credit position in the balance sheet. Rum goings on though they are. Neither do I have much to say about the serial entrepreneurial owner to whom this accounting black hole was unknown. Save to quote his response to the accusation he was thinly spread, 'fair challenge'. I will note the rapid capital raising and loans to the company he put in place. Thereby saving, at least at the time of writing, several thousand of his employees' jobs.

Instead, my observations are twofold: the first fold is the design of the company's ownership and the second fold is stellar performance.

Of the first fold. This company is set up in the supposed best way to minimise conflict between the aim of the company and that of the owners. The observed conflict as discussed earlier is that executives will feather their nest at the cost of shareholders.

Well, the design of PV has the executive Chair owning a large percentage of the company. And, that stake in turn being a large percentage of the Chair's personal fortune. What conflict could exist between the aims of the owner and the aims of the business? What could possibly go wrong?

This designed in lack of conflict is often held up as showing why PLCs fail. And why, for instance, the mutual model of member owned building societies and insurers is superior. In investment banking terms the Goldman Sachs of partnership days being a superior form to the listed Goldman Sachs of today.

Well. No. Effectiveness is the key not design. If design was the key to success 25% of UK building societies would not have been rescued from failure during the Great Financial Crisis. And, the mutual insurer Equitable Life would not have failed in 2000.

Let me elaborate. Here is a design question, beloved of the tick box approach to corporate governance. Is there a board risk committee whose members are all non-executives? Tick yes, tick no.

Here is the effectiveness question: are the firm's key risks understood and managed well?

Turning to the second fold, stellar performance. You may recall my earlier story about Harry:

*We make a mistake when we only interrogate the numbers in brackets. There is great danger when the board says: "thank God for Harry, he always delivers".*

No-one goes to look at how Harry is producing results until it is too late. If the name had been Nick we could have thought Leeson and why Barings celebrated his profits but never troubled to understand how this was possible. In the end they came to understand that there were no profits, only catastrophic losses.

PV produced great results, a darling of the markets but now it appears that there may have been a Harry or Nick involved. It appears no-one thought to ask how the darling results were possible.

We will look at the difference between design and effectiveness in a later chapter. But, for the moment, let me say that effectiveness is to design as 80 is to 20. And, with special reference to incentives. Never celebrate the winners stellar results without understanding how they do it.

Before we get to what should a NED do about incentives we have to go a little further with the research. This means examining four sorts of incentives: extrinsic, intrinsic, financial and non- financial.

Read on!

---

1. The Kay Review Of UK Equity Markets And Long-Term Decision Making—Final Report July 2012 4 The Kay Review Of Uk Equity Markets And Long-Term Decision Making—Final Report July 2012
2. Compensation Committees and CEO Compensation Incentives in US Entrepreneurial Firms—Conyon and He 2004
3. Ibid.

# 36

# EXTRINSIC AND INTRINSIC INCENTIVES

E xtrinsic incentives are provided as a reward to the job holder by some third party, typically an employer. Extrinsic rewards may be financial, non-financial or both. In contrast, intrinsic rewards derive from the job itself as described by Amabile:

> ... *the importance of intrinsic motivation: the motivation to work on something because it is interesting, involving, exciting, satisfying, or personally challenging. There is abundant evidence that people will be most creative when they are primarily intrinsically motivated, rather than extrinsically motivated by expected evaluation, surveillance, competition with peers, dictates from superiors, or the promise of rewards.*[1]

An important word to pick up on here is creative. Senior executives and especially CEOs have to be creative. They need the ability to manage ambiguity, face simultaneous challenges, see through to the fundamental issues, arbitrate on wicked problems and then design and drive for the requisite change.

Designing change and working out the right set of objectives to drive the organisation is a highly creative endeavour.

The problem is that intrinsic incentives, necessary for creativity, seem to be inhibited by extrinsic incentives. Jobs where extrinsic incentives work well are likely to be those of a routine nature where there is little intrinsic reward, these tend not to be leadership roles.

*Decades of strong evidence make it clear that large performance-related incentives work for routine tasks, but are detrimental when the task is not standard and requires creativity.[2]*

The following diagram captures this:

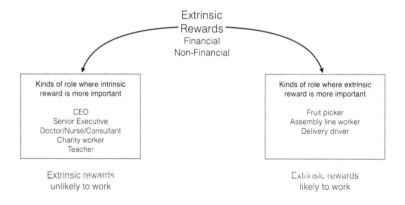

NEDs and Trustees often think hard about extrinsic rewards when designing bonus schemes but do they think about the impact on the very thing they need most, creativity in their senior people? If a CEO's rewards are heavily skewed to EPS and ROE don't expect much else. Reward A, and B becomes a forlorn hope. The creative talents of the CEO will focus on the finance based performance proxies you have put in place.

All of this tends to lead to extremely complex schemes.

Whilst it is said that what gets measured gets done it is also true that:

> ... *anything that can be measured and rewarded will be gamed.*[3]

The more complex the scheme the more difficult it will be to administer and to spot attempts to game it.

An example of gaming was described to me by a bank's non-executive director in the course of researching this book.

The bank concerned had a portfolio of lending, within which was a large poorly performing loan. There was eventual agreement with the executives that a write-off would take place at the half year and then a bigger write-off at the full year. This would impact the executive bonus pool and was therefore a tricky discussion, but credit to the non-executives, they stuck to their guns. At the full year the non-executives noticed that although the loan had been written down as planned there was no reduction in the bonus pool. On investigation they found out that the loan had been re-classified in the bank's books as a held for sale asset rather than a loan in the normal course of trading. The executive bonus pool was not impacted by write downs of held for sale assets.

The final point here is a question posed by Cable and Vermuelen:

> *Perhaps you think you have to offer a large percentage of variable pay to help your firm attract top executives. Even if that is true, think about who will be attracted to such a package: the very people most in need of a financial incentive to work hard and perform well.*
>
> *Are you sure those are the people you should want to attract in the first place?*[4]

I am not presenting an argument against bonuses. I am presenting an argument that NEDs need to think about how incentives are triggered well before a debate over how much the incentive should be.

1. Motivating Creativity in Organisations: On Doing What You Love And Loving What You Do—Teresa M. Amabile
2. Harvard Business Review—Stop Paying Executives for Performance by Dan Cable and Freek Vermeulen—FEBRUARY 23, 2016
3. Muller, Jerry Z. The Tyranny of Metrics Princeton University Press 2018 2018 ISBN 978-0-691-17495-2
4. Harvard Business Review—Stop Paying Executives for Performance by Dan Cable and Freek Vermeulen—FEBRUARY 23, 2016

# 37

# FINANCIAL AND NON-FINANCIAL INCENTIVES

I f we start by following the money, all financial rewards are extrinsic and there is a fairly short list:

- Salary
- Bonus
- Commission
- Pay progression
- Overtime
- Piece work

Apart from salary all need some sort of proxy for the quality or amount of work done to trigger a payout. As we now know, the issue with proxies is that they focus attention on a subset of the role leaving other parts of the role, which may be crucial to success, open to chance. A point made by Dilbert:

*Pointy Haired Boss—your compensation will be based on achieving these goals*

*Dilbert—awesome, it's like written permission to ignore everything else you ask me to do*[1].

Using financial measures such as share price, EPS and ROE as the proxy can lead to all sorts of undesirable behaviour, as explained by Warren Buffett in his 2005 letter to shareholders:

> *Too often, executive compensation in the U.S. is ridiculously out of line with performance. That won't change, moreover, because the deck is stacked against investors when it comes to the CEO's pay. The upshot is that a mediocre-or-worse CEO – aided by his handpicked VP of human relations and a consultant from the ever-accommodating firm of Ratchet, Ratchet and Bingo – all too often receives gobs of money from an ill-designed compensation arrangement.*[2]

Going on to describe such an ill-designed scheme Buffett highlights the possibilities for executives:

> *Take, for instance, ten year, fixed-price options (and who wouldn't?). If Fred Futile, CEO of Stagnant, Inc., receives a bundle of these—let's say enough to give him an option on 1% of the company—his self-interest is clear: He should skip dividends entirely and instead use all of the company's earnings to repurchase stock.*[3]

Writing about share buy backs in the FT in 2014 Edward Luce pointed out that CEOs persuading other stakeholders to support stock repurchase is a feature of poor corporate governance:

> *The more immediate culprit is the decline in the quality of corporate governance. The average tenure of the US CEO is falling. Buying back shares instead of investing makes sense if you do not expect to be around for the pay-off. It is a no-brainer if you measure the time horizons of most executive reward packages ... Their incentives are skewed towards*

*extracting value from the companies they run, rather than creating future value.*[4]

The truly crackers point to all of this is that research by the High Pay Centre shows no link between pay and profit/EPS.

*... the statistical correlations between changes in two key annual bonus performance metrics, pre-tax profit and earnings per share (EPS), and subsequent bonus payments were insignificant*[5].

To hammer the issue home here are three points from the report:

- 98.7 per cent of the change in annual bonuses could not be explained by changes in pre-tax profit:
- 99 per cent of the change in annual bonuses could not be explained by changes in EPS:
- there was no noticeable correlation between the relative ranking of long-term incentive plan (LTIP) share awards and the relative ranking of changes in total shareholder return over three years:

The coup de grace is unequivocal:

*... there is little discernible link between directors' earnings and corporate performance.*[6]

Does this imply removing financially targeted bonuses? This is code for salary only schemes. Before we get to that contentious point we should understand, in agreeing to a performance based incentive scheme, NEDs are faced with four choices:

| Choice 1: Fixed versus variable (Required for all schemes) | How much of the scheme is fixed salary versus variable performance bonus? |
| --- | --- |
| Choice 2: Performance proxies (Only required for variable performance bonus schemes) | Are the metrics that trigger payments financial (EPS/ROE), Environmental/Sustainable/Governance (ESG) measures or a mixture? |
| Choice 3: Payment form (Only required for variable performance bonus schemes) | What proportion of the bonus is paid in cash versus market linked instruments such as shares and share options? |
| Choice 4: Deferral period (Only required for variable performance bonus schemes) | Is the bonus payable immediately it has been earned or is payment deferred for a period? |

What is immediately obvious is that a salary only scheme is far easier to administer because Choices 2, 3 and 4 fall away. If there is a variable pay element to the scheme there is no option but that all of Choices 2, 3 and 4 apply.

A good question is whether these choices are conscious decisions of the NEDs or default positions because 'we've always done it this way'. Pictorially, the four Choices could look like this where X marks the spot chosen by the NEDs:

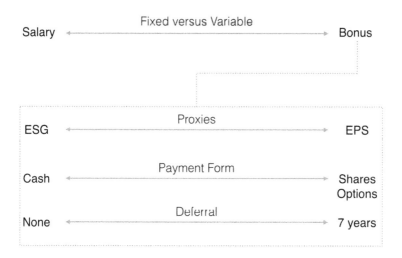

I have chosen 7 years on the deferral scale as this is the maximum deferral in the UK for bank bonus schemes. Obviously if there is no regulatory requirement NEDs are free to consider other time periods.

In the case of Universities, Hospitals and Charities there is no 'EPS" option and the payment form is bound to be cash. However, if the 'EPS' absence is replaced by 'hit budget' the problem is much the same.

The four choices all have different risks and it is worth working through each to sort out what these are.

Starting with fixed versus variable, as with all of the choices, NEDs have a range of options·

Choice  1 - Fixed versus Variable

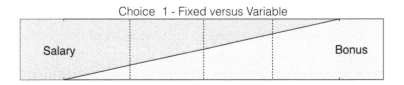

At the salary end the issue is that recipients have no incentive to take risks and can sit back and enjoy the ride. If results are poor then so what, the pay just rolls on in. With any element of bonus, the risk is that the proxies chosen to drive payout will be the sole focus of recipients, even if this generates risk to the business. The incredibly important point here is that it is not the size of bonus relative to salary that matters. Whether the bonus is 5% of salary or 255% of salary what triggers behaviour is what triggers the bonus. It is the bonus triggers that influence behaviour not the amount triggered.

Mitigation is generally done by arriving at some mid-point combination of fixed and variable pay. Which mid point is chosen is the $64,000 question, pun intended. Many CEO schemes are well to the right of the mid point, with bonus high in comparison to fixed salary.

The advantage of the pure salary end of the scale is that creativity of the CEO and other executives is not constrained by any focus on proxies required to trigger variable pay.

The next choice to consider contains the performance proxies that drive variable pay, remembering this only applies if the scheme contains a variable bonus:

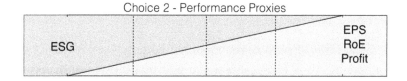

Choice 2 - Performance Proxies

Here the choice is between ESG measures and measures linked to the organisation's financial performance.

Throughout both parts of this book we have noted the toxic impact market based measures can have on organisations through short term risk taking—do whatever you can to improve the share price. ESG by comparison appears to encourage long term thinking.

> *High Sustainability companies are more likely to have established processes for stakeholder engagement, to be more long-term oriented, and to exhibit higher measurement and disclosure of non-financial information. Finally, High Sustainability companies significantly outperform their counterparts over the long-term, both in terms of stock market and accounting performance.*[7]

There is a current debate on what proportion of bonuses should be linked to ESG measures, 30% or 50%. There does not appear to be any question about 100%. In contrast there are still many schemes totally linked to market based rewards.

Choice 3 is how the bonus will be paid out. This is shown below and again this only applies to the variable bonus element of a scheme.

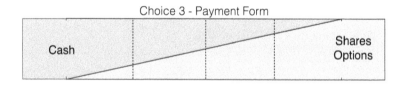

The form of payment is important because even if Choice 2 comprises 100% ESG, paying out in share options brings focus on the share price back into the scheme.

Combining Choice 2 EPS/profit with Choice 3 payment in share options/shares leverages the CEO/executives focus on the share price enormously.

The fourth and final choice is deferral through malus and clawback, again applying only to variable bonus.

Deferring variable pay, usually for a number of years is to prevent short term reward with no account taken of losses that arise later. Malus and clawback are components of deferral explained in the figure below.

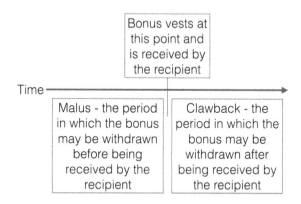

The theory is that only when both malus and clawback periods have passed is the bonus irrecoverable. Whilst on the face of it deferral is a good approach it suffers from a major flaw, that of 'stacking'.

The executive over several years will accumulate a 'stack' of shares/options which will be at different points on the malus/clawback timeline. This stack will build up and become worth far more than the current year's bonus. Consequently the impact of market price movements on the 'stack' will be of much more interest to the executive than any form of curtailment of the current year's bonus. This is not a fresh discovery:

> *For example, a CEO may receive 100,000 options this year, which might add to 400,000 options granted in previous years, for a total of 500,000 options held. If the stock price decreases, then the value of the 100,000 options granted this year declines —but so does the value of the options accumulated from previous years. Since the CEO will care about the whole stock of 500,000 options, not simply this year's 100,000, executive compensation received in any given year provides only a partial picture of CEO wealth and incentives. To understand CEO incentives fully, it is important to focus on the aggregate amount of shares, restricted stock, and stock options that the CEO owns in the firm[8].*

It is clear that the impact of 'stacking' could well be a short term incentive to chase the share price upwards, which is a considerable headwind to efforts to incentivise for the long term good of the firm.

However, there is a strong counter argument that having at least the CEO tied to a deferral period, say the UK 7 years, means that this will extend beyond the time the CEO leaves the organisation. In which case the CEO is reliant on the long term health of the organisation and of course the quality of the next generation of executives.

In concluding financial incentives let me return to that question of whether to get rid of bonuses in favour of salary only.

It's not like this is a new idea. Some banks have removed financial incentive targets from their front line employees precisely because of the poor behaviours these had encouraged. Examples are UK banks following the PPI miss-selling scandal and Wells Fargo in the US with its own scandal of phantom account opening. The question is whether ExCo incentives have also been removed. Defending financial incentives on ExCo whilst removing them from the front line ought to be the ultimate irony. Sauce, goose and gander spring to mind.

From a NED perspective a salary only scheme removes the overhead of managing short term incentives but then has issues at both extremes of the performance scale. If results are poor, beyond a 'good talking to', NEDs have no intermediate step of reducing or removing a bonus before finally sacking the CEO. At the other extreme if the firm performs out of its socks then there is no financial upside for the CEO.

The difficult question is whether these issues are worth it for the removal of short termism. The advantage of no 'extrinsic' pressure on executives' creativity is a risky theory for NEDs to prove in practice.

The challenge of shareholder vested interests to such a change would be immense. Whilst shareholders do protest against huge and/or easy to achieve executive bonus schemes I do not recall any protest against bonuses per se. However, there is no denying that a salary only scheme would redefine the type of person willing to take these roles on.

The best guidance for NEDs is they need to make four conscious choices and that they should start with the profile of the CEO they wish to attract. That profile of course being defined by the purpose of the firm.

These four choices NEDs make set out Kerr's A by definition and B by non-definition. By definition you reward A, and what you don't reward is B. NEDs must know what is in B and to what extent they value that. Bear in mind that in most cases it is a forlorn hope B will get substantive focus in competition with A.

These incentive choices profoundly affect the way the business is led and thus knock onto culture through how or if the *Purpose* is delivered. This is also a big influence on the perceived trustworthiness of senior leaders.

1. Dilbert Wednesday 28th November 2012
2. Berkshire Hathaway Inc. 2005 Annual Report.
3. Ibid.
4. ft.com—Edward Luce—The short sighted US buyback boom—22nd September 2014
5. Executive remuneration in the FTSE 350 – a focus on performance-related pay—October 2014—A report for the High Pay Centre From Incomes Data Services
6. Ibid.
7. The Impact Of Corporate Sustainability On Organizational Processes And Performance—Robert G. Eccles Ioannis Ioannou George Serafeim— Working Paper 17950 http://www.nber.org/papers/w17950
8. Executive Compensation and Incentives Martin J. Conyon—2006

# 38

# SETTING INCENTIVE SCHEMES

I n following the money a key issue is who signs off extrinsic incentive schemes. It is clearly the role of NEDs on the remuneration committee to set the CEO's pay. The question is to what extent they are involved in setting others pay?

NEDs who do not involve themselves in the design of pay schemes throughout the organisation are taking the risk that schemes 'invisible' to them will encourage the wrong behaviours. Let me illustrate this by returning to the chain of command we used for communications:

CEO
|
ExCo
|
Middle Management
|
First Line Management
|
Workforce

This chain of command is generic across industry sectors: public, private and charities. The differences between organisations are only the number of layers of middle management. All of these roles are important as far as driving behaviour is concerned.

What drives poor behaviour is often lack of board oversight in the way roles below the CEO are extrinsically rewarded. The diagram below illustrates this:

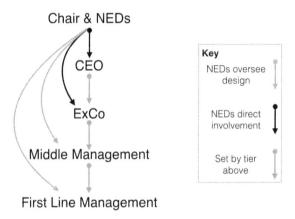

The NEDs via the black arrows have a direct involvement in setting not only the CEO's pay but also that of the CEO's direct reports. As shown by the grey arrows the NEDs also have oversight of how pay schemes are designed further down the organisation, preferably as far as the first level managers. First level managers are incredibly powerful drivers of front line behaviour and it is a risk to have their pay schemes subject to no NED oversight. By NED oversight I do mean signing off the Executives' pay policies for the organisation and having some means of gaining assurance these are being adhered to and work. The assurance usually being by Internal Audit.

Down the centre the orange arrows denote the other extreme. This is where the NEDs have no involvement beyond setting the

CEO's pay. All other pay is set by the CEO or by the management tier above. This is a big risk in terms of behaviour as it allows an errant CEO a free hand with rewards.

If NEDs do not have a say in pay policies throughout the organisation and a means of assurance then I'm afraid they are inviting both prudential and conduct risk to crystallise.

# 39

# NON-FINANCIAL INCENTIVES

H aving followed the money I will now turn to non-financial incentives. Non-financial rewards derived from the job itself are intrinsic. However, recognition is extrinsic and takes many forms.

A good way to understand recognition is to ask one of the shortest questions in the English language: who is? People watch what their bosses do and say, and also what they don't do and say, so answering this question is crucial.

Who is?

Fired
Promoted
Not believed
Excommunicated
Believed    Not fired
Not hired  Hired  Celebrated
Not promoted  Denigrated  Ignored

These are powerful forms of recognition.

Who is fired, hired, excommunicated, promoted, celebrated, ignored, not fired, not hired, not promoted and denigrated are all powerful determinants of behaviour.

A feature of the way people watch and listen to their bosses is the speed of the communication process. The straight arrows drawn in the figure above show this. There appears to be no frictional impediment, the message passing quickly and seamlessly.

These 'who is' questions are pointers to the corporate culture. They reflect the behaviour of the board, in other words the behaviour of the NEDs themselves. This is an important aspect of tone from the top. For instance, the way senior executives get paid is a test of how NEDs set the tone from the top. 'Who is celebrated' is an interesting question if the CEO gets a bonus despite poor corporate results.

Whilst it might appear I am straying back to financial incentives who gets what is a form of recognition. The CEO and EDs with defined benefit pension schemes which for everyone else have been withdrawn and replaced by defined contribution schemes. More simply, ExCo receiving an 8% salary rise while the workforce get 1%. I'm not arguing for equality, I am arguing for understanding the impact of decisions like these, made by NEDs on RemCo. They determine who gets recognised and who does not.

The Buffett example of fixed price options is also the responsibility of the NEDs on RemCo. They have the mandate and should have the ability to design sound pay schemes. They should also have the will to resist the blandishments of the CEO and advisers.

The 'who is' question is not only a matter of who gets celebrated. It is also reflective of which functions in an organisation are important. 'Who is' can occur in an organisation that sets out to, but fails to deliver, fabulous customer service. This may be because resources: people, products and/or processes are insufficient. Then employees will see that *Stated Purpose* versus *Purpose-in-practice* is a double standard. This is highly damaging to trust in senior leaders.

The cultural impact worsens in this organisation which purports to be a service oriented business if promotions and recognition only go to sales people. Rewarding A in this way leaves B a forlorn hope.

To conclude, as I said above I am not arguing for equality, mind you, I'm not arguing against it either. I am arguing for the need to understand the impact of decisions that seemingly are only about the CEO and ExCO. They are not. These decisions are in the end broadcast, because most of them wind up in disclosures in the report and accounts. Make whatever decisions you like about recognition, but please, as you make them step back and think about impact.

# 40

# SUMMARISING INCENTIVES, WHAT CAN NEDS DO?

With regards to incentives, I can't blame anyone for asking, what on earth can NEDs do in the face of all this?

The answer is be aware and be resolute.

Be aware that whatever scheme is put in place defines both A and B and that an eye needs to be kept on the B that is not incentivised. And, however carefully a scheme is designed it can only be a proxy for performance, especially in senior roles that are full of ambiguity. Also, be prepared for gaming.

NEDs don't need to be experts on Intrinsic and Extrinsic rewards, but knowing that creativity can be blanked out by extrinsic rewards is of itself valuable. It should make NEDs think more carefully about extrinsic rewards and what measures they are based on.

NEDs should use the four choices as a debating tool amongst themselves when designing at least the CEO's pay package. Where you land on the dimensions fundamentally sets out the sort of person who will be attracted to the CEO role. However, the start point is not the pay package. The start point is what sort of person do you want to lead your business? Once that is established then the pay package dimensions should be aligned with that profile.

Just to illustrate the point, here are two different choices, X1 and X2 where X marks the spot. I will leave it to you to work out the different sorts of people you are likely to attract as CEO and the consequent impact on the culture of the firm.

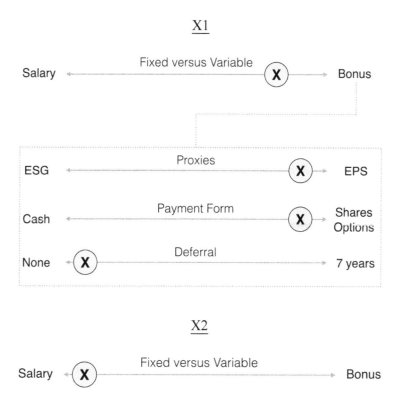

The same discussion should also be had by NEDs about the form of pay scheme for other senior executives. X2 for instance accurately describes the pay scheme for NEDs, fixed with no performance bonus. But, ask yourself, should X2 also describe the heads of the independent control functions in risk and audit? In similar vein should X2 describe the package for the General Counsel?

I make no judgement here other than these questions need to be the subject of a conscious, serious and researched debate resulting in a set of decisions approved by the NEDs. Bear in mind, as with the CEO, the start point is not the design of the pay scheme, it is the profile of the people you want to attract so as to reinforce the culture needed to meet the organisational *Purpose*.

What else NEDs can do is watch for the development of extremes in senior executive pay, especially to stand up against CEO pressure to change the design of schemes for personal benefit. The extremes of pay include rewarding poor performance and, just as we discussed in the risk chapter, NEDs must use stress testing. Ask, what could the maximum payout be?

*The size of the awards, in excess of ten times the average for a FTSE 100 Chief Executive, and the fact that performance was so clearly affected by Government policy rather than the actions of the executives, suggest that this was about as clear a case of an inappropriate pay package as one could imagine.*[1]

Finally, NEDs must oversee incentive schemes throughout the organisation. This is achieved by setting out clear policies of what is acceptable and what is not. It is important that NEDs use their mandate to audit the schemes on a regular basis, through HR and/or Internal Audit.

In summarising this chapter, the most essential take away is the challenges NEDs face in scheme design, measuring true performance, being prepared to deal with under-performance/bad behaviour and resisting unscrupulous attempts by executives to feather their nests.

This aspect of the NED role, setting and monitoring incentives, is at the heart of culture because the choices made fundamentally impact the CEO's behaviour. This inevitably influences the culture and thus behaviour throughout the organisation.

There is a concluding fair warning to NEDs from Muller:

*It is simple-minded to assume that people are motivated only by the desire for more money, and naive to assume that they are motivated only by intrinsic rewards.*[2]

In the end it is about integrity and on that subject I will close our discussion on Culture and what drives behaviour with another quote from the sage of Omaha:

*"Somebody once said that in looking for people to hire, you look for three qualities: integrity, intelligence and energy. And if they don't have the first, the other two will kill you. You think about it: it's true. If you hire someone without integrity, you really want them to be dumb and lazy."*[3]

---

1. BEIS Select Committee Inquiry on executive pay: High Pay Centre response—May 2108
2. Muller, Jerry Z. The Tyranny of Metrics Princeton University Press 2018 2018 ISBN 978-0-691-17495-2
3. Thoughts of Chair Buffett—Simon Reynolds—Harper Business

# 41

# IT'S LEADERSHIP NOT GOVERNANCE

No-one leaps out of bed in the morning, breathes deeply and cries: 'today I am going to govern corporately'. Corporate governance is not inspiring. However, given *breathe* is the root of the word inspire let us breathe life into corporate governance by recognising it for what it is: leadership.

When people think of leaders they think of individuals. But, organisations are led by a group, such as the board of directors or trustees. This group, the board, serves one purpose which is to successfully lead the business. As individuals, the different members of the board have various roles and in effect provide each other with checks and balances which should enable the group to take key decisions well. Emphasis there on the word should. 'Should' is dependant on how effectively these individuals work together. The elusive and much sought after board effectiveness is at the heart of this.

The board is not some alternative life form that somehow is or is not effective. It is a group of people. Their effectiveness or ineffectiveness as a team emerges from how they interact with each other.

My use of the word team is deliberate. Team is often bandied about to describe any small group of people without any real thought given to what a team is. Back in 1993 Katzenbach and Smith[1] wrote engagingly about the difference in performance between various types of working. It is a useful high level model for calibrating board effectiveness because it talks about purpose, performance and accountability.

Just before you say team? Board? Never in this world. Please reflect. Whatever description is used you will find that what is needed is cohesiveness around purpose, performance and accountability. And it's not a new idea because team was used by Sir Adrian Cadbury to describe his view of the board back in 2002:

*Boards are teams and like other teams need to be made up of people with different attributes.*[2]

The Chair, the CEO and the Board are about leading the business and as such have a direct effect on corporate culture.

We will therefore park corporate governance and look instead to corporate leadership.

1. Wisdom of Teams—Jon R. Katzenbach & Douglas K. Smith, Harvard Business School Press, 1993
2. Corporate Governance and Chairship a personal view–Adrian Cadbury OUP 2002

# 42

# CORPORATE LEADERSHIP

With all this in mind I reckon the Great Financial Crisis of 2007/8 was preceded by a catastrophically bad period of corporate leadership. Commenting on this we have the opening paragraph of a G30 report in 2012:

> *In the wake of the crisis, financial institution (FI) governance was too often revealed as a set of arrangements that approved risky strategies (which often produced unprecedented short-term profits and remuneration), was blind to the looming dangers on the balance sheet and in the global economy, and therefore failed to safeguard the FI, its customers and shareholders, and society at large.*[1]

The counter argument to my 'catastrophically bad' thesis is that these failures could not have been foreseen by boards who were overcome by external causes such as: macro-economic instability, poor regulation and bad political decisions.

The answer of course is that these external causes did apply in 2008, but to try and argue that boards had nothing to answer for in the run up to the crisis is to deny the facts. Moreover, as put by the Chair of the 1984 Federal Inquiry into the failure of Continental Illinois we must be able to cope with all seasons:

> *The list of excuses will be long and varied. Some will tell us the economy did it. I was as concerned as anyone about the recession but it is far too simplistic to let the economic downturn be used to paper over the deficiencies at Continental. We must have a banking system and a regulatory system for all seasons—for good times and bad times*[2].

In the grand tradition of not learning from history we find similar comments nearly thirty years later when the UK Parliamentary Commission looked into the failure of HBoS:

> *No bank is likely to be immune from the effects of an economic downturn, but the scale of HBOS's credit losses was markedly worse than that of any of its major peers ... an apology is due for the incompetent and reckless Board strategy: merely apologising for having failed to plan for an unforeseeable event is not much of an apology.*[3]

And bringing ourselves right up to date we find this said about the failure of Carillion in 2018, which before its collapse was the second largest construction company in the UK:

> *... the collapse of Carillion was, to them* [the board], *the fault of their advisers, the Bank of England, the foreign exchange markets, Brexit, the snap 2017 General Election, Carillion's investors, Carillion's suppliers, the entire UK construction industry, Middle Eastern business culture, the construction market of Canada, and professional designers of concrete beams.*[4]

In addition to accountability, we should also wonder about

the importance of subject matter expertise amongst members of the board.

The regulator's inquiry into the failure of RBS records this of Fred Goodwin's right hand man, Johnny Cameron. Goodwin had entrusted oversight of RBS's US investment bank to Cameron who asked the head of that, Brian Crowe, about the US investment bank's business:

> Cameron - 'how much leakage of sub-prime into CDO business?' Crowe - 'CDO is all sub prime related'

Cameron went on to say to the regulator:

> 'I don't think, even at that point, I fully, I had enough information. Brian may have thought I understood more than I did ... and it's around this time that I became clearer on what CDOs were, but it's probably later.'[5]

Ignorance of subject matter was not unique to RBS, it is also highlighted in the failure of HBoS:

> The non-executives on the Board lacked the experience or expertise to identify many of the core risks that the bank was running.[6]

And of course we have already noted similar issues at both Kids Company and Mid Staffs NHS Trust:

> ... a complete lack of experience of youth services amongst Trustees[7].

> The [NHS] Trust Board leadership between 2006 and 2009 was characterised by lack of experience ...[8]

Corporate governance sets the leadership framework of the organisation and it ought to be no surprise that expertise is a key part of the effectiveness of boards. How is the purpose of the organisation settled, the strategy to achieve that purpose agreed and the organisation led through thick and thin to achieve it if none of the NEDs/Trustees sufficiently understand the core business?

Neither should we be amazed that expertise is a key driver of the behaviour of the board, both as individuals and as a group. As we know, behaviour describes in large part the culture of an organisation. An organisation led by a board collectively ignorant of the fundamentals of the business makes a very clear cultural statement.

I mentioned in the introduction to the Second Part that *ensuring general wisdom* is cracking shorthand for the role of the NED. Wisdom it appears is at the heart of governance, as Sir Adrian Cadbury describes:

> *Governance is a word with a pedigree that dates back to Chaucer and in his day the word carried with it the connotation wise and responsible, which is appropriate.*[9]

Wisdom is generally described as the intersection of knowledge and experience, it's a bit difficult therefore to see how wisdom can be ensured with no or little subject matter expertise amongst the NEDs.

Finally, returning to accountability, the US Inquiry into the causes of the great financial crisis found refusal of this a common theme:

> *The Commission heard testimony from the former heads of Bear Stearns, Lehman, Citigroup, and AIG, among others. A common theme pervaded the testimony of these witnesses:*
> *We were solvent before the liquidity run started.*

*Someone (unnamed) spread bad information and started an unjustified liquidity run.*

*Had that unjustified liquidity run not happened, given enough time we would have recovered and returned to a position of strength.*

*Therefore, the firm failed because we ran out of time, and it's not my fault.*

*in each case, the CEO was willing to admit that he had poorly managed his firm's liquidity risk, but unwilling to admit that his firm was insolvent or nearly so. In each case the CEO's claims were highly unpersuasive.*

Corporate leadership is about purpose, performance and accountability. Ensuring this is delivered by the executive is the role of the Chair and NEDs who must themselves collectively possess enough subject matter expertise to understand the business, enabling them to challenge and support the executive as necessary.

In concluding this section here again is Sir Adrian Cadbury quoting from a 1928 government report on the subject (my emphasis):

*The truth is that a strong and possibly efficient management rather likes to have an ineffective Board which will __know too little__ to have views or to interfere: and the ineffective Board enjoys its fees.*[10]

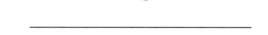

---

1. Toward effective governance of financial institutions - G30 - 2012
2. Inquiry into Continental Illinois Corp. and Continental Illinois National Bank - Hearings before the Subcommittee on Financial Institutions Supervision, Regulation and Insurance of The Committee on Banking, Finance

and Urban Affairs, House of Representatives - Ninety-Eighth Congress Second Session September 18, 19 And October 4, 1984

3. House of Lords House of Commons Parliamentary Commission on Banking Standard 'An accident waiting to happen': The failure of HBOS Fourth Report of Session 2012-13

4. House of Commons Business, Energy and Industrial Strategy and Work and Pensions Committees—Carillion—16 May 2018

5. The failure of the Royal Bank of Scotland
   Financial Services Authority Board Report—December 2011

6. House of Lords House of Commons Parliamentary Commission on Banking Standard 'An accident waiting to happen': The failure of HBOS Fourth Report of Session 2012-13

7. House of Commons Public Administration and Constitutional Affairs Committee—The collapse of Kids Company: lessons for charity trustees, professional firms, the Charity Commission, and Whitehall—Fourth Report of Session 2015–16

8. The Mid Staffordshire NHS Foundation Trust Public Inquiry—Chaired by Robert Francis QC—Vol 1 page 139—February 2013

9. Cadbury, Adrian. Corporate Governance and Chairship: A Personal View. OUP Oxford.

10. Cadbury, Adrian. Corporate Governance and Chairship: A Personal View. OUP Oxford ... quoting from Britain's Industrial Future—Ernest Benn—1928

# 43

# DESIGN AND EFFECTIVENESS

################

B efore we get to the 'how' of corporate leadership we must understand the difference between design and effectiveness. Our introduction is provided by Justice Owen who led the Royal Commission into the failure of HIH Insurance:

> *"... the expression 'corporate governance' embraces not only the models or systems themselves but also the practice by which that exercise and control of authority is in fact effected".* [1]

Justice Owen differentiates between the theoretical framework and the practice of corporate governance. The 2012 G30 paper on effective corporate governance explained this in a different way:

> *Behaviour appears to be key, and a focus on right behaviours means a shift from the "hardware" of governance (structures and processes) to the "software" (people, leadership skills, and values)......The software makes the hardware function.* [2]

You will notice that it is behaviour that is described as key, which of course in setting out culture at the top of the organisation is exactly right.

I am not a fan of *hardware* and *software* in the context of corporate governance. I prefer *design* and *effectiveness* being more descriptive of what we are about. Here are four examples.

| Design | Effectiveness |
|---|---|
| Is there a board risk committee? | Is risk understood and managed well? |
| Is there a Chief Risk Officer? | Is the Chief Risk Officer able to give an expert view to the NEDs independent of management? |
| Do the board minutes record the corporate plan as being signed off by the board? | Were NEDs given time to critique the plan, what changed as a result? |

A moment of reflection might reveal that effectiveness is more difficult to assess than design.

For example, establishing the design point that a firm has a chief risk officer (CRO) can be discovered from an organisation chart. However, this organisation chart, beautifully clear though it may be, cannot tell you about effectiveness: that for instance the line of business heads have no respect for the CRO. Neither will it reveal how the CRO's behaviour influences the behaviour of the risk department. As is seen here at Washington Mutual it can be malign:

> ... one of the senior vice presidents in WaMu's risk department, instructed risk managers to "shift (their) ways of thinking" away from acting as a "regulatory burden" on the company's lending operations and toward being a "customer service" that supported WaMu's five-year growth plan[3].

Establishing the effectiveness of the CRO is clearly very different and more difficult than simply establishing the role exists in the structure.

Effectiveness questions need more experience and time to answer. For instance, 'is risk understood and managed well' is not a function of 'is there a risk committee'. I have seen plenty of small organisations where, unable to afford a Chief Risk Officer, the Finance Director double hats as the head of risk and the Audit Committee does double duty as the Risk Committee. These organisations are often well able to understand and manage their risks. In the exact opposite, I have seen global organisations possessed of an independent CRO and Risk Committee, with slide deck polished risk frameworks designed by global consultancies, that are very shaky when it comes to understanding and managing their risks.

I also know NEDs who have been on their board several years over the nine year UK limit, yet who remain thoroughly independent and constructively challenging. I have also come across NEDs who have been only months on a board but who will never be able to challenge their way out of a wet paper bag.

In a nutshell, design is easy, there is a risk committee tick the box, whereas effectiveness is not only harder but may well reflect on a director's character and reputation. NEDs should not ignore design but rather see any poor examples as amber warnings since poor design may compromise effectiveness.

Let me illustrate this amber light point by returning for a moment to the small organisation whose audit committee double hats as the risk committee. NEDs simply need to understand one risk to this set up lies in quarters 1 and 4 of the organisation's financial year. In these quarters all audit committees are focused on working with the external auditors to sign off the report and accounts. It is therefore quite likely that the risk agenda will be lost or at least suppressed in the face of the race to close the accounts. It does not mean this is not do-able, it just means NEDs need to spot the amber warning, understand the risk and watch out for it.

Boards themselves are designed in different ways and it is a reasonable question to ask whether this impacts effectiveness. Let's therefore take a look at three examples: the UK Unitary, the

European Two-Tier and the US 'Presidential'. These are shown below:

The UK Unitary board meets in the same place at the same time. All of the non-executive directors and executive directors share the same board papers and packs of information.

The European Two-Tier board has the executive directors and non-executive directors sitting on separate boards that generally meet apart from each other and may well have different sets of board papers.

The US 'Presidential' board has the role of the President/Chair/CEO assigned to one person who is often the only executive on the board. This President has a major role in recruiting the NEDs.

Given these brief descriptions I ask seminar groups I teach which one they would assess as the weakest from an effectiveness standpoint. Invariably the answer is the US model, it being assumed the powerful President/Chair/CEO will rule for ill rather than good. At which point I mention Walmart, Intel,

Apple, GE and ask whether these commercial success stories indicate poor board effectiveness. In comparison, the corporate failures we have already discussed: HBoS, RBS, Carillion, Mid Staffs NHS Foundation Trust and Kids Company all had unitary boards.

This is a further clue that design, whilst important, is not as vital as effectiveness. If anything this reminds us again that the 'board' is not a person, it comprises a group of people. It is the effectiveness of the individuals working as a group under the leadership of the Chair that we are looking to determine.

This leads neatly into that territory beloved of consultants and governance gurus, the board effectiveness review.

1. HIH Royal Commission. The failure of HIH Insurance—ISBN 0 9750678 5 0 (set)—April 2003.
2. Toward effective governance of financial institutions - G30 - 2012
3. The Lost Bank: The Story of Washington Mutual-The Biggest Bank Failure in American History by Kirsten Grind

# 44

# BOARD EFFECTIVENESS REVIEWS

W hy? Why review boards? One answer is why wouldn't you review what you do? Additionally, in the UK, is the expert analysis of the Walker report which recommended:

*The board should undertake a formal and rigorous evaluation of its performance, and that of committees of the board, with external facilitation of the process every second or third year.* [1]

Unfortunately, there is evidence that this type of review is not delivering. Spencer Stewart, a firm who undertake reviews on behalf of boards, have had this to say:

*Despite their growing adoption, board assessments are falling short of their promise of enhancing board effectiveness in some cases. Boards that take a compliance-oriented approach — or structure the process in a way that prevents a true examination of the impediments to board effectiveness — lose the opportunity to gain valuable shared insight into the operation of the board and ways to improve its composition, processes and relationships.* [2]

In my own view we are discussing the effectiveness of the board effectiveness review no less. Too often reviews land around point A in the figure below. As opposed to where the value lies, and where the elephant in the room sits, at point B.

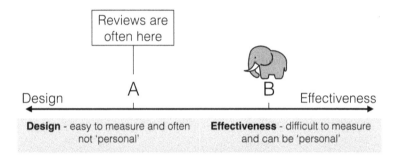

There appear to be two reasons for this.

First. As we have already seen, measuring design is easier than measuring effectiveness. This ease of observation means it is easier to establish the health of the design side. Measuring effectiveness is more difficult. This is why a lot of reports land their conclusions on design issues. Not only is design easier to measure but there are no behaviours involved. This means there are no difficult 'what do we do about that elephant sat over there' type discussions.

Effectiveness is more difficult. Not because it is harder to observe but because it needs skill and trust to get honest and open views on the table. The elephant question. The doubt about someone's personal effectiveness. This needs careful broaching and tactful handling.

The second reason for A being the more likely landing place than B is our old friend, principal-agent. Who is conducting the review? Whoever, is likely to be the agent of, in the UK, the Senior Independent Director (SID) or the Chair of the board. If the board effectiveness roots in a failure of the Chair and/or SID, then this is a huge elephant in the room. Which means there may well be a tendency for the reviewer to pull punches. After all, an external reviewer will have an eye to future business. As well as wanting a good reference for other business. If an under performing NED is on the board of a valued client of the reviewer this is another conflict of interest.

Even when the review is internal there are principal agent problems. Consider the impact of giving adverse feedback on personal career prospects. This is not a trivial challenge for a General Counsel or Company Secretary given the task.

Managing the output is one thing, Managing the input is another. The scope agreed by the NEDs with the reviewer is key. Is anything or anyone off-limits?

On the scope point remember that one of the four drivers of culture is decision making. So, how effective is the board at making those few important decisions? This is an important consideration. There has to be a question over the review if it does not interrogate how the board made a key decision. If this is not done it is difficult to see how the effectiveness question can have been answered.

Finally, of course is the big so what? A completed report presented to the board and discussed. Then what? The sixty four thousand dollar question is what happens because of the report?

I have concluded that board effectiveness reviews are only ever as good as the Chair of the board. We can expect the best Chairs to be open to feedback and encourage the reviewer to be frank. All with an eye to improving the effectiveness of the Chair and the board. We may expect something different of those Chairs who are at least part of the problem. They might not be open to the feedback needed to make a difference. Spencer Stewart allude to this when they talk of engaging *board leaders* in the review:

> *Should board leaders be assessed? Our experience is that the board's effectiveness is impacted directly by the board's*

*leadership. Even though the Chair is guiding the process, the best situation is when that person is open to feedback about his or her leadership.*[3]

The final issue is the challenged Chair receiving the draft report about the Board. This is then 'adjusted' to taste before discussion with the other directors.

You can criticise me for casting aspersions but I am not describing the 'minority report'. I have read many reports and this is not idle supposition. We pretend if we work on the belief the effectiveness of an effectiveness report is not open to massage.

There is no simple solution and the conclusion that these reviews do not add value is wrong. However, NEDs have to recognise the potential issues. Then they must get involved in transparent debates about design, effectiveness and elephants.

---

1. A review of corporate governance in UK banks and other financial industry entities - November 2009 - Walker
2. https://www.spencerstuart.com/research-and-insight/improving-board-effectiveness-five-principles-for-getting-the-most-out-of-a-board-assessment
3. Ibid.

# 45

# A BOARD OF EXPERIENCED DIRECTORS

I f the measure of board effectiveness is how well it makes key decisions then is NED experience an important ingredient? Well, let us test the answer to that question by looking at the failure of Royal Bank of Scotland.

That the Board were experienced is without doubt. The figure below graphically records the other organisations the NEDs were directors of in 2008, all blue chip profit and not for profit firms.

The RBS board, at least tacitly, agreed to a number of high risk activities. Taken independently these might have been manageable but taken together they comprised a very significant threat.

This is all confirmed in the report on the failure of RBS by the board of the UK Financial Services Authority (FSA):

> *While external factors were undoubtedly important in RBS's failure, banks are run by people and those in board and senior management positions are responsible for the decisions they make. It is only with hindsight that it is clear that there were specific decisions taken by the RBS Board and senior management which placed RBS in a more vulnerable position than other banks when the financial crisis developed between 2007 and 2008.*[1]

And so we must ask: how is it a board of experienced directors can go on to make a series of judgements that proved to be catastrophically bad for the business?

One of the challenges the RBS board undoubtedly faced when considering the ABN takeover was the success their executive experienced with a previous takeover, that of the RBS takeover of NatWest. It is easily forgotten that in 2000 RBS was three times smaller than NatWest but not only succeeded in the takeover of its bigger rival but also in the subsequent activity to integrate the two businesses. Fred Goodwin, the RBS CEO at the time of the 2008 collapse, was the RBS number two in 2000, but it was his perceived success as integrator of the two banks that helped confirm his reputation.

Years after the NatWest acquisition the RBS board were roundly criticised for their lack of due diligence of the ABN takeover:

> *Many readers of the Report will be startled to read that the*

*information made available to RBS by ABN AMRO in April 2007 amounted to 'two lever arch folders and a CD-rom: and that RBS was largely unsuccessful in its attempts to obtain further non-publicly available information*[2].

However, the same report also records in interview Johnny Cameron, Fred Goodwin's number two at RBS:

'One of the things that went wrong for RBS was that, and I say this to many people, we bought NatWest as a hostile acquisition. We did no due diligence. We couldn't because it was hostile. After we bought NatWest, we had lots of surprises, but almost all of them were pleasant. And I think that lulled us into a sense of complacency around that. The fact is that the acquisition of ABN was also hostile. We got bits and pieces of information but fundamentally it was hostile. There's this issue of did we do sufficient due diligence. Absolutely not. We were not able to do due diligence...that was part of doing a hostile acquisition.'

A conclusion may be that the board of RBS drew a sense of comfort from the past success in taking over and integrating the much bigger NatWest. This is interesting because we find Daniel Kahneman counselling against drawing such comfort:

Leaders who have been lucky are never punished for having taken too much risk. Instead, they are believed to have had the flair and foresight to anticipate success, and the sensible people who doubted them are seen in hindsight as mediocre, timid, and weak.

A few lucky gambles can crown a reckless leader with a halo of prescience and boldness.[3]

RBS is an example of a board with a good experienced background. One could be forgiven for thinking the board would be able to mitigate the risks in the business as well as the risks in undertaking a huge acquisition, even as markets globally became very difficult. That the board was not able to mitigate either the business as usual risks or the execution risk of the ABN acquisition shows that assuming effectiveness can rest on the experience of the board is not wise.

Lehman Brothers appears to be at the other end of the scale as evidence to the US Financial Crisis Inquiry Commission revealed in 2011:

> *Nell Minow, editor and co-founder of the Corporate Library, which researches and rates firms on corporate governance, raised other reasons that observers might have been sceptical of management at Lehman. "On Lehman Brothers' [board], . . . they had an actress, a theatrical producer, and an admiral, and not one person who understood financial derivatives[4]."*

It is therefore clear that both experienced and inexperienced boards have problems with judgement and although it is right to populate a board with experience, and to make sure this includes the right expertise, this is not anything like a complete defence against failure.

Thus we have further confirmation that effectiveness wins out over design. However, we can't ignore design, it being my view that effectiveness is to design as eighty is to twenty.

All of this leads to the big questions of what do NEDs need to do and stop doing? Well, we should start with challenge, as everyone seems to agree that challenge is the thing that NEDs need to excel at.

Let's find out if it is.

1. The failure of the Royal Bank of Scotland Financial Services Authority Board Report - www.fsa.gov.uk/rbs December 2011
2. Ibid.
3. Thinking, Fast and Slow by Daniel Kahneman
4. Final Report Of The National Commission On The Causes Of The Financial And Economic Crisis In The United States Submitted By The Financial Crisis Inquiry Commission -21 January 2011

# 46

# CHALLENGE BY NEDS IS ONLY HALF THE STORY

W hen reviewing the role of the NED in 2003 Higgs said this:

> *Non-executive directors need to be sound in judgement and to have an inquiring mind. They should question intelligently, debate constructively, challenge rigorously and decide dispassionately. And they should listen sensitively to the views of others, inside and outside the board.*[1]

It is clear then, that before the crisis, NEDs were expected to challenge. Which begs a big question, why didn't they? An important contribution in the UK came 'post crisis' in 2009 from the Walker Review with this comment on the process of decision making:

> *The sequence in board discussion on major issues should be: presentation by the executive, a disciplined process of challenge, decision on the policy or strategy to be adopted and then full empowerment of the executive to implement.*[2]

Significantly, Walker went on to say:

*The essential "challenge" step in the sequence appears to have been missed in many board situations and needs to be unequivocally clearly recognised and embedded for the future.*

NED challenge is therefore well established, at least in theory, which leaves us with the question why in practice it didn't happen in the run up to 2007/8. Here, in two stories, may be the start of an answer.

Directly related to NED challenge is the question of 'do the NEDs need to know?' This was answered for me by an ex-trustee of a national UK charity who I met whilst researching this book (a trustee performing the role of NED in a charity). When fairly new in role she had asked the charity's executive for some specific information. On being told this was not information for trustees, she reverted to the board Chair. The Chair backed the charity executive and put this information off-limit the trustees. In the end, in fairly short order actually, this trustee resigned.

Trustees and NEDs cannot have any information in the firm 'off-limits' and so resigning was one of two correct responses. The second correct response would have been to dig in and decide that over the term of appointment the Trustee would work hard to change this culture, to get the other Trustees onside and push the Chair to a different and right place.

The wrong answer of course would be to stay on the board and do nothing, which is a neat link to my second story.

A failed firm's board minutes revealed a NED, on first arriving, asking many questions about the margin. After a few months these interventions ceased to appear in the minutes. Following the failure of the firm (due to the collapse of the margin) the NED was asked what had happened, why did he stop challenging the executive? The answer was that the Chair had a word with the NED saying the questions were not seen as helpful by the

CEO and other NEDs, and so the NED stopped asking and stopped confronting the issue. Given no-one else was tackling the problem the executive escaped challenge on this key point. The NED was wrong, as was the Chair.

During a debate into board governance it was notably declared: *Every director should have an answer to the question: "What would it take to make me resign[3]?"* Compare the two stories.

Challenge by NEDs is difficult: requiring not just clear thinking to decide that a particular challenge is necessary, but perseverance and resilience to see the challenge through to a conclusion. The importance of the Chair of the Board is obvious. A Chair who is not prepared 'to call a CEO out', allowing NEDs to make challenges, renders board challenge and by extension the board itself ineffective.

A key personal conflict facing NEDs is their own principal-agent challenge. All NEDs have to take account of the impact on their own reputation and remuneration if they are seen to be 'awkward'. As Carl Icaan the activist shareholder commented:

> *"If you give a director hundreds of thousands in board fees a meeting and all kinds of perks, he doesn't have a lot of incentive to see that come to an end."*[4]

NEDs will not only bear in mind what they have to lose by way of remuneration and status, but also how their reputation may be perceived by other firms looking to recruit NEDs. It takes personal resolve to resign from a board and few will exercise this option lightly.

A further example of where challenge went wrong can be drawn from debacles at the Co-operative Group and Co-operative Bank in 2014. These resulted in the Group losing control of the Bank which led to a review of governance at Group level by Lord Myners. He noted that:

*Lay directors repeatedly blame management as almost entirely responsible for the Group's failures. With very few exceptions, lay directors do not admit to their own failings, including their consistent inability to exercise proper oversight of management.*[5]

Lay directors had arisen as a peculiarity of the democratic process within the Co-op Group. Acting in the role of NEDs these were people with no previous senior level commercial experience. Neither did they possess relevant expertise. It might therefore be thought they are not representative of professional NEDS, which is largely true. However, they provide at the extreme a clear example of how not to perform the NED function.

Myners went on to helpfully describe the fully functioning board, and here he helps fill out an important part of Walker's axis between unquestioning support and unconstructive challenge:

*The key task of the board is not, as believed by some on the Group Board and in the wider Co-operative Movement, to "control" management. Rather, a good board plays a multiplicity of leadership roles—some highly visible but others quite subtle—from setting strategic direction to overseeing risk management to providing challenge, guidance and support to management.*[6]

At this point we have confirmation of the substantive roles of NEDs but Myners goes on to cover another highly important role NEDs play, supporting the CEO:

*For chief executives, one of the most valuable—and valued— roles that a board can play is to provide counsel and mentorship. Responsibility for leading a large organisation is, in fact, a lonely job and chief executives often have few people to turn to for candid and thoughtful advice. This suggests not only that the board must possess the experience, perspective and wisdom that would be useful to the chief executive but that the relationship between them needs to be underpinned by trust and mutual respect[7].*

There is further confirmation from Sir Adrian Cadbury:

*Chief executives should be able to see their boards as a continually available source of counsel and support, rather than mainly as a monitor and paymaster.[8]*

Counsel, mentorship, trust, mutual respect are all crucial to the role of the NED. But, never forget that other reason for the existence of NEDs which is to hold the executive to account. It is at the heart of the 'pretend conversation' I had with the bank NED.

This interplay between challenge and support can be thought of as an axis as in the figure below:

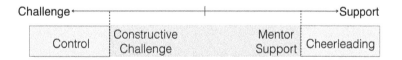

Between the two extremes (control and cheerleading) is the territory NEDs will most often inhabit: constructive challenge alongside mentoring and support. It is not the case that the extremes in grey are bad and the central themes in blue good, for there are good and bad behaviours attaching to all four as the next two tables show.

Firstly, examples of good behaviour:

| Control | Constructive Challenge | Mentoring and Support | Cheerleading |
|---|---|---|---|
| Replacing an underperforming CEO | Critiquing the corporate plan to improve it | Supporting the CEO when a risk crystallises | Supporting an investor roadshow |

It may be thought odd that firing a CEO is good behaviour, the CEO is unlikely to think so. However, to put up with under performance in this key role and not to tackle such a crucial issue has a dire impact on the firm's culture. Behaviourally, it amounts to painting in large friendly letters over the main entrance of head office: 'it's OK around here to be rubbish at your job'. Dealing with executive under performance is a critical aspect of the NED role in developing the culture of the firm.

It is also true in reverse that familiarity can breed contempt. An excellent paper from the NHS Foundation supports Dame Onora O'Neil's observation that too much trust can be a bad thing:

> *In the interviews, board members also argued that inappropriately high trust could discourage members from actively questioning issues or seeking further information. One Chair said: "There is a sense of comfort in the executive directors by the non-executives, developed through confidence that has built up over the past few years. However, this can sometimes lead to insufficient scrutiny which needs to be managed."*[9]

As regards examples of poor behaviour it is too simplistic just to reverse the good behaviours. It is better to look more thoughtfully as shown below:

| Control | Constructive Challenge | Mentoring and Support | Cheerleading |
|---|---|---|---|
| Dominating and acting as an executive | Constantly criticising the executives on minor matters | Undermining individuals | Supporting a culture that refuses to accept bad news |

As regards control, NEDs are not executives and the Chair or any other NED has no place dominating executives or regularly forcing through decisions. Similarly, constant criticism is unlikely to bring out the best in the executives, it is more likely to result in avoidance tactics by the CEO and executives such as not bringing issues forward to the board. By undermining individuals I mean such as congratulating to the face whilst stabbing in the back. Finally, not allowing bad news to surface is toxic. The core of a healthy culture in any organisation is that it can accept and deal with bad news either from the 'shop floor' or from outside the firm. The board must encourage that conversation: 'boss I have bad news, the ugly truth is ...', and then, with no shots being fired at the messenger, permit the ugly truth to be recounted in all of its ugly detail. This is a key part of trust and communication, two of the four drivers of culture.

The relationship between the NEDs and the Executive needs to sustain the business. That argues for avoiding the extremes except in unusual circumstances whilst more usually collaborating through constructive challenge, mentoring and support.

The balance to my good behavioural point about replacing an under-performing CEO is that the Chair and NEDs do not rush there without trying to get to the bottom of the under-performance. Just replacing the CEO without an attempt to support and improve performance is pretty one dimensional although in the end it may be the right decision. It is a fine balance.

This behavioural discussion is not supposed to lull anyone into thinking that a good board will always exhibit good behaviours. Given a board is a group of people, each with their own personal motivations, troubles and frailties, any idea that somewhere out there is a Nirvana of jolly collaboration is flawed. Apart from anything else most of us have experienced socially weak super intellects: the one with the social skills of a bull elephant and the other the assertiveness of a nervous mouse. Pile on top of that the usual ebb and flow of human emotion and the role of the Chair in steering the board is seen for what it is, challenging.

The figure below is stylised but attempts to show how a good board will still have its moments.

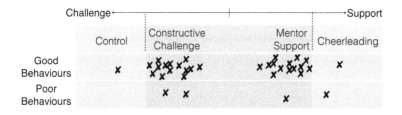

One of the key roles of the Chair is to make sure the overall temperature of the board is under control. If poor behaviour amongst the non-executives assumes the ascendancy this will encourage poor behaviours amongst the executives on and below the board. For instance, and as mentioned before, constant criticism and aggressive handling of papers and presentations by the non-executives will lead to the executives massaging input to the board to curry favour by suppressing bad news.

Clearly the opposite applies and a CEO who is allowed to manipulate and dominate the board should be challenged. If the Chair is not prepared to do that then the CEO and fellow executives have a fairly clear path to capturing the firm.

Reflecting on the financial crisis where challenge was poor there has always been the danger of a pendulum swing and challenge becoming synonymous with non-executives, it is all they should do. It clearly isn't and balance is key.

A clue to another of the building blocks of effectiveness is the size of the board. The 2012 G30 report into board effectiveness has this to say:

*A board of 10 to 12 members can operate efficiently, cohesively, and decisively. It is also easier to get input from everyone if the board is smaller, and smaller boards tend to be more intimate and comfortable with candour. On larger boards, bad news tends to stay just below the surface. Making just this point, one Chair observed, "The bigger the crowd, the better the news[10]."*

It was also covered by Lord Myners in his review of the governance of the Cooperative Group in the UK:

*Boards should be large enough to ensure that the skills and experience required by the business are present but not so large as to make board meetings unwieldy and diminish the ability of individual directors to contribute meaningfully. Various studies, including previous UK reviews of co-operative governance, have concluded that boards should ideally have no more than 8 to 12 members.[11]*

In considering the importance of the size of the board I suggest you just consider the dynamics of time. If you are a director on a board of twenty versus being a director on a board of ten you are bound to have half the chance to speak and inter-vene on the larger board where twice as many people have to be heard. Moreover, the loud and insistent voices will always be heard relegating some directors to silent, possibly passive-aggressive 'acquiescence'. Equal to this is the danger that turning up as a passenger and not contributing is made that much easier on the bigger board.

The final damnation of the large board is the increased load on the Chair who has that many more directors to keep in touch with between board meetings, as well as a much multiplied 'ebb and flow of human emotion' which we talked of earlier.

1. Review of the role and effectiveness of non-executive directors–http://www.ecgi.org/codes/documents/higgsreport.pdf
2. A review of corporate governance in UK banks and other financial industry entities - November 2009 - Walker
3. Think-tank searches for good governance. By Peter Whitehead - ft.com http://www.ft.com/cms/s/0/18549298-e94a-11e2-bf03-00144feabd-c0.html?siteedition=uk#axzz2kkBeCN1q
4. Financial Times—29/12/2013—http://www.ft.com/cms/s/0/0b1ecc28-6f06-11e3-9ac9-00144feabdc0.html#axzz2yB883zV5
5. The Co-operative Group—Report of the Independent Governance Review —Paul Myners 7 May 2014
6. Ibid.
7. Ibid.
8. Cadbury, Adrian. Corporate Governance and Chairship: A Personal View. OUP Oxford.
9. Effective boards in the NHS?—A study of their behaviour and culture—NHS Confederation—2005
10. Toward Effective Governance of Financial Institutions - G30 - April 2012
11. The Co-operative Group—Report of the Independent Governance Review —Paul Myners 7 May 2014

# 47

# THE WILL, THE SKILL AND THE KNOWLEDGE

I challenged myself on challenge, is this the only quality needed? In the end I found three NED qualities: the will, the skill and the knowledge.

The will is no more nor less than taking on principal agent. Being able from time to time to adopt a contrarian position. If needed, to be the most unpopular person in the room.

The practical challenges to NEDs of exercising 'the will' are legion:

'if I challenge I might get a reputation as one of the awkward squad, which might get back to headhunters, which might compromise my chances of future NED appointments' ... 'if I resign this is even more nuclear, my reputation will definitely be on the line and very likely damaged' ... 'no-one else challenges' ... 'there's no point, I've tried many different ways and the Chair always takes the CEO's side' ... 'I would like to be re-appointed for a further term and so I must not upset the Chair' ... 'I don't think it is my part to say anything, I am Non-Executive not Executive' ...'I'm only part time'.

We mentioned above the critical role of the Chair of the board. The Chair must be clear, by actions not words, that constructive challenge is welcome. Then the will of NEDs to challenge will emerge.

On its own, having the will to challenge is not enough. Which takes us to the skill: knowing when to challenge, and how to challenge.

Knowing when to challenge brings to mind the axis we spoke about earlier. The skill of when to move from mentoring and support into constructive challenge. A feature of which is how often to play this card. Because, as mentioned, constant criticism is not a positive but a negative.

An effective challenge is not one written up in the board minutes. 'Mr Sutherland robustly challenged the corporate plan' is dross. A skilful challenge steers a debate through action. It neither writes for the file nor embarks on a personal attack. In other words an effective challenge makes a difference. Ask, what changed as a result of the challenge?

Again NEDs face practical difficulties:

> 'I keep on losing the plot when I challenge' … 'I can't help getting cross about this' … 'I know the answer is there somewhere but I can't see the wood for the trees' … 'I keep on talking detail' … 'I know I keep fighting too many battles' … 'I'm sure the Chair is going to have a word with me, I'm always on about this' … 'no matter how many times I raise this I still don't get a clear answer' … 'any issue I raise is seen by the CEO as a personal attack'.

The Chair has a central role in helping NEDs choose when to challenge and the best way to challenge. There is great danger in a losing a valid challenge because of poor NED skills. It is too easy for challenge to appear personal, or even if it is not, to be taken that way. It bears repeating that the Chair has a vital role here: recognising an inexpert challenge, defusing emotion and retaining it for examination by the board. As vital is the private discussion afterwards with the inexpert NED of a better way next time. It takes little imagination to reflect on the reverse. The Chair who closes the challenge down in the boardroom and afterwards criticises the NED for being disruptive.

Finally, knowledge or expertise. If the NED lacks knowledge of the business, or has no access to other NEDs with knowledge of the business, then challenge will be weak. It is important to stress that we are talking about the collective knowledge of the NEDs. It is reasonable to expect that a bank will have some NEDs with relevant banking experience. That does not mean every NED on a bank board has to be an ex-banker any more than every NED on a hospital board has to be an ex-medic.

Please also note the use of the word relevant. Working for a life insurer thirty years ago is not the relevant background for a 21st century general insurer.

The practical challenges in not having the knowledge are for example:

> 'every time I raise a challenge the CEO has impressive rationale, facts and figures which overwhelm me' … 'I keep on looking foolish and no-one backs me up'… 'although this is not my specialist subject I know something is not right' … 'there is no-one else on the board who can help me' … 'none of us NEDs know enough about this business' … 'the jargon loses me'.

A senior Chair summed up knowledge for me by asking: *how do you challenge without understanding?* This happily sits alongside my response to those who have said to me: 'ah but John, I am able to ask the stupid questions'. In reply I ask: 'are you also able to spot the stupid answers?'

Given the Chair is crucial to the effectiveness of the NEDs, is having 'the knowledge' mandatory for a Chair? None of Northern Rock, RBS or HBoS had bankers as Chairmen. The Kelly Review into the debacle at the Co-op Bank in 2014 has this to say about that bank's Chair:

> *Despite the amount of time he appears to have devoted to the role, his lack of relevant financial services experience and knowledge meant that he was ill-placed to advise, challenge or performance manage the Bank CEO - still less to give the Bank strategic direction at a time of great difficulty.*[1]

It isn't possible to be definitive because no firm is the same and situations differ and have their own context. Having said which, let us say I jump into a Chair's shoes. Please suspend disbelief. Let us also say it is as Chair of a pharmaceutical company, an industry of which I have zero experience. How comfortable am I? Not very. For market knowledge, strategy development and risks I would have to rely on others, executive and non-executive. The Chair should not be executive but my lack of experience would be not be a handicap but would of itself be a risk.

I don't doubt I will now be given a host of really good examples contradicting this so let's leave it as a risk issue. If you feel the Chair's lack of knowledge is a risk to the business that can be mitigated then I will not argue. I will argue if you haven't recognised it as a risk and worked out in practice how the mitigation will work. And, by the way, 'in practice' means in war-time as well as in peace-time.

The will, the skill and the knowledge is the core of constructive challenge and support. NEDs with this core are more able to move their business forward. Much more able than those who pretend.

Another key dynamic is time. Having the will, the skill and

the knowledge is of little use to NEDs if they only meet a few days a year.

This issue of time is a major source of dispute. Very often I have had it put to me that a NED working many days a month or full time in an organisation becomes Executive. This makes no sense to me at all. The two roles are entirely different. It is not time spent in the firm that determines whether a person is executive or non-executive. In fact, if I'm honest, whenever I hear a NED say "but I'm not executive" I immediately think they're copping out.

These are facts: businesses are more interconnected, the pace of change is high, disruption of business models continues apace. Thus it is inevitable that pressure on NEDs will increase. And, the one way the pressure manifests itself is in the amount of time needed to do the job.

Another demonstration of lack of time is the firms where the board meets six or even less times a year. I have experienced this. It is hard to keep track of a business with two month gaps between meetings. I was relieved when the board recognised this problem, going to ten longer meetings a year. I am not advocating long meetings but I do support giving NEDs the time to debate important issues. It is also challenging trying to pick up what happened two months ago as it is covering key and complex matters in a short meeting.

Where boards meet four or six times a year it is a clear signal to me that the board is ineffective. It may be convenient for the CEO and executives but the NED role in these circumstances is in danger of being symbolic, to the point of being ceremonial.

This is the rub. What is the point of your board, what is its purpose? Would it be missed if it didn't meet at all except to ceremonially sign off the accounts once a year?

Board meetings have to be regular enough for the NEDs to meet and develop relationships between themselves and the key executives in the business. In my view this is at least eight times and preferably ten times a year.

The great reason for an organisation having an informed and constructively challenging group of NEDs working under the leadership of a good Chair is to improve the judgements made by the executives. The NEDs are not there to make the executives lives miserable but to help them deliver a commercially successful business. None of this is possible if meetings are few and far between.

Returning to what Higgs said in 2003. He described the NED role encompassing four elements: Strategy, Performance, Risk and People:

- **Strategy**: *Non-executive directors should constructively challenge and contribute to the development of strategy.*
- **Performance**: *Non-executive directors should scrutinise the performance of management in meeting agreed goals and objectives and monitor the reporting of performance.*
- **Risk**: *Non-executive directors should satisfy themselves that financial information is accurate and that financial controls and systems of risk management are robust and defensible.*
- **People**: *Non-executive directors are responsible for determining appropriate levels of remuneration of executive directors and have a prime role in appointing, and where necessary removing, senior management and in succession planning.*[2]

If we want to see effective boards then we must have effective NEDs. That emphasises the need for NED mastery of the will, the skill and the knowledge. Not forgetting to add the key dimension of enough time to do the job effectively.

1. Failings in management and governance—Report of the independent review into the events leading to the Co-operative Bank's capital shortfall —Sir Christopher Kelly 30 April 2014
2. Review of the role and effectiveness of non-executive directors—Derek Higgs January 2003

# 48

# DOMINANT PEOPLE

I once asked my own Chair what he did, what his role was mainly about. He said he had three big responsibilities: that he must choose the next CEO, ensure the board was effective in leading the business and, in the end, help choose his own successor.

He also said that choosing a CEO is a defining point, a decision which sets the direction and culture of an organisation for years ahead. He added he would generally get one chance to get this right.

Remembering this conversation took me to thinking about the kind of person a CEO needs to be. Short listed candidates are unlikely to be shrinking violets, more likely there will be a collection of dominant individuals. With the evidence of the damage the 'brooks no dissent' type of dominance can wreak it does raise a question: is this right? Are dominant people right for the role of CEO and, if they are, is there a special sort of dominance that is OK?

CEO dominance can be channelled by the wise words and actions of the Chair and NEDs. Conversely, the dominance could be let rip in a destructive manner if the Chair and NEDs are weak.

However, the idea that dominance is bad, so have the Chair and NEDs blunt or suppress it just kept nagging away at me. Why recruit this characteristic at all? The breakthrough for me was reading a paper by Tang, Crossan and Rowe:

*Somewhat like financial options ... powerful boards may keep the downside risk of having dominant CEOs under close control while leaving the upside potential relatively open. It logically follows that powerful boards will increase the likelihood of having sound versus unsound strategic deviance and thus the likelihood of having big wins versus big losses. Thus, the effect of dominant CEOs on firm performance is more positive when the board is powerful than when it is less powerful.*[1]

In other words a dominant CEO can be influenced when the Chair and NEDs are powerful in their own right and this is likely to improve the chances of a good result and reduce the chances of a poor result.

You will remember the discussion earlier in the book on strategy and the key relationship between the NEDs and CEO. For ease of reference the diagram illustrating this is below:

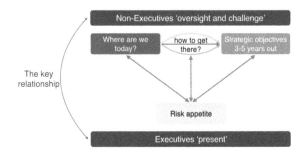

There are supportive points made by Tang et al here. In

effect, that a powerful board will put more effort into assessing the CEOs strategic proposals, furthermore, that the powerful board will be capable of throwing out any ill thought through proposal. Additionally, the example set by the Chair and NEDs leads to better quality work by the CEO and management team:

> ... *facing a powerful board,* [the management team] *will become more diligent and thus exert more effort in the strategy initiation process and thus weed out unsound strategic deviance by itself.*[2]

I'm behind this idea that dominance is a force for good as well as the often assumed force for ill. It also reinforces the role of the Chair and NEDs as a countervailing force for good. But, the effectiveness of that force for good depends on the power of the group relative to the power of the CEO. I illustrated this relationship earlier when discussing decision making using the following diagram:

| Powerful NEDs ← | CEO | → Weak NEDs |
|---|---|---|
| Non-Executives Impact Positive | | Non-Executives Impact Negative |
| Constructive challenge Mentoring and support Open and transparent interactions Open and respectful CEO Strong control functions | | Challenge weak/suppressed No mentoring or support Information flow difficult, interaction fraught CEO dismissive/'hard to read' Intimidated control functions |
| Speaking Up likely to thrive Decisions broadly based | | Good news only Narrowly based, brooks no dissent |

It is worth noting a few collateral effects. If there is a powerful group of NEDs expect powerful and independent control functions (General Counsel, Risk and Internal Audit). Equally, staff will feel more confident about speaking up safely. And, it is a given that the key decisions the board makes will be broadly based on the collective intellect of the whole board, non-executives and executives.

The comparison of a weak Chair and NEDs is stark.

We have debated at some length what NEDs have to do to be effective, in summary the will, the skill and the knowledge. We also need to accept that this is not a one way street because the CEO, dominant or not, cannot just be a free riding passenger when it comes to behaviour.

If domination is allied to such poor behaviour by the CEO that, for instance, good people depart leaving behind a diminished and cowed ExCo, then you are well into the 'brooks no dissent' kind of territory that we have seen cause so much damage. The most fundamental challenge the Chair and NEDs have to handle is when a highly performing CEO is also a behavioural monster. If this goes unchallenged by the NEDs because the results look good then the road ahead is to perdition.

Another challenge would be that of incentives. As discussed previously a reward hungry CEO, with the fulsome support of a remuneration consultant and the HR Director may put forward a scheme that runs opposite to what the NEDs agree is needed. But, as with the behavioural monster, the financial performance is stellar and the market loves the CEO. The owners of the business might be quite keen on the financial results and relatively disinterested in how these are achieved.

These are serious challenges for NEDs who must bear in mind that short term results from behavioural monsters and bonus hunters are likely to be allied to a poor culture. In the end it will be the NEDs who have to clear up the mess.

A hidden feature of CEO dominance is that it tends to increase the longer the CEO is in role. This is simply down to the rotation of NEDs off the board. As this experience disappears and new NEDs are on-boarded the CEO gradually becomes the most experienced person in the board room, as far as knowledge of the business goes. This knowledge can become a bar to constructive challenge.

This is not an argument for CEOs being in role for short periods, there are plenty of examples of long standing CEOs who have performed extraordinarily well. It is simply a statement of fact and Chairs forewarned about this are better able to manage the risk.

There is then the question of collaboration. Some CEOs view NEDs as a form of threat to their authority, others of course are open, collaborative and helpful. If NEDs are going to be able to give maximum help to their CEO there is need for the business complexity to be simplified for them. This has to be done by the full time executive led by the CEO which is of course at the collaborative end of executive behaviour. Remember Andrew Bailey's wise words about the haystack:

> *Non-Executives should not be left to find the answers for themselves, and they should not feel that they have to do so out of a lack of sufficient confidence in what they are being told. In other words, they should not be pointed towards the haystack with warm wishes for the search ahead.*[3]

It is not enough for the CEO led executive to be helpful or collaborative, they need to ensure complex matters are described as simply as possible so that NEDs can more easily engage in the debate. This act of simplification is in itself a developmental challenge for the executives. It is entirely true that to teach a subject you have to really understand it and this mastery of understanding will help the executive as much as the NED.

Of course the foundational developmental experience for the CEO and ExCo is in deciding that it is to their advantage to do this at all.

In enabling the non-executives to challenge more easily the executives may, from time to time, make their own lives uncomfortable. However, really effective Chairs, CEOs and NEDs see each other as critical friends whose experience and knowledge is a means of improving judgement.

It is obvious, if the Chair and NEDs can improve the decisions of the CEO and executive directors then everyone prospers.

Which observation takes me on to the last leg of our corporate governance journey, the role of the Chair of the board. I'll segue in with another quote from Cadbury:

> *The responsibility for ensuring that boards provide the leadership which is expected of them is that of their Chairmen.*[4]

---

1. Dominant CEO, Deviant Strategy, and ExtremePerformance: The Moderating Role ofa Powerful Boardjoms_985 1479..1503Jianyun Tang, Mary Crossan and W. Glenn Rowe—Journal of Management Studies 48:7 November 2011 doi: 10.1111/j.1467-6486.2010.00985.x
2. Ibid.
3. Governance and the role of Boards—Speech given by Andrew Bailey, Deputy Governor, Prudential Regulation and Chief Executive Officer, Prudential Regulation Authority—Westminster Business Forum, London 3 November 2015
4. Cadbury, Adrian. Corporate Governance and Chairship: A Personal View. OUP Oxford.

# 49

# PRIMUS INTER PARES

I f corporate governance is corporate leadership then first amongst equals is the Chair.

Early on I stressed the importance of a good cadre of informed NEDs led by a good Chair. This is the best support executives can have in guiding their own personal success. The tragedy is the extent to which this goes unrecognised. Worse, that some executives see informed NEDs as a form of threat.

Take a CEO with a defensive approach, one that does not lead to collaboration with the NEDs. In the end the strong Chair, with the NEDs, will find a different CEO. On the other hand the weak Chair will not correct the CEO. As this CEO's power increases the effectiveness of the board will deteriorate.

There are many descriptions of an effective board. Including collaborative, diverse, challenging and commercially aware. Yet, when it comes to board effectiveness there is one ultimate measure. The quality of the key decisions the board makes. So, all the efforts of the Chair need to focus on honing this collective skill.

Common themes crop up when you ask Chairs how they measure their own effectiveness.

There is leading oversight of strategy and performance plus guiding and challenging management. Also, whether the board is as harmonious and efficient as it could be.

Chairs also worry about their own knowledge. One described the 'factual bucket', do I know enough about this subject, if I don't what is the risk and who do I ask?

One mentioned chairing a board of high quality but bloody difficult people. Another, on a listed board, remembered the first time running an AGM. Almost the shock of being more in the public eye.

None of this should be a surprise. Chairs are not magicians and will be subject to the same doubts as anyone else. In fact if they aren't then that is a bit of a worry. The over weaning self confidence exhibited by some CEOs is not going to be well managed by a Chair with the same qualities.

One point that came out repeatedly was the need for Chairs to listen. Not to dominate board discussions. The skill of inviting the executives to set out the context of a board paper. Then, after listening to directors' views, sum up to conclude with a good decision. Wonderfully intellectual debate may be enjoyed by one and all. But, if the board puts off key decisions or constantly gets them wrong then the whole point of the board is lost.

An interesting theme is about engagement with NEDs and the CEO outside the boardroom. Several times I heard of engaging with board members between meetings. This included two different themes, one supporting the CEO and the other the NEDs. But the interplay was in binding both together.

In the case of the CEO the Chair needs to spend time ensuring this usually dominant figure 'gets' what bothers the board.

With the NEDs, the challenge is to build great collegiality. NEDs must feel that they can challenge the executive without the risk of a slap down or being ignored. Especially, that they can challenge each other.

The Chair is centre stage in leading a culture in which challenge can thrive. This means the whole board, executive and non-executive, understand that challenge improves judgement.

It is also up to the Chair to help executives understand that NED challenge, not always being right, is a good thing.

The Chair has a major leadership role to play in instilling confidence in the NEDs. They must have the will to challenge. A good Chair is also able to help NEDs develop the skill to challenge. And a good Chair will make quite sure the collective knowledge of the NEDs is up to the task.

Choosing the board agenda is also top of mind. The struggle to stop the agenda taking over the board. Key subjects the board needs to take its time over being squeezed out. The idea of a top ten list came up a few times as a way Chairs kept an eye on this.

On culture I heard that values on a wall and a lift don't mean a thing. It is drivers of behaviour that influence culture. The way people are paid and how they are appraised and recognised were commonly seen as key drivers.

We have discussed the importance of the will, the skill and the knowledge. These NED qualities are even more important for Chairs. But, the Chair having the will, skill and knowledge is not enough. The board is not going to advance far if there is not a high quality supporting cast of NEDs. A key part of this, in the hands of the Chair, is succession planning.

Too often the succession plan can be non-existent, or if existent not workable or adhered to. I have seen cases where 'all of a sudden' several NEDs are due to retire in short order. This is compounded if it includes the Chair. Of course it never should be 'all of a sudden' because NED appointments are for multi-year stints.

The Chair must have a clear view of when NEDs are due to be renewed or retired. Also, what their collective experience and skill looks like. There is no justifiable reason for bad planning.

The succession plan will start by focusing on knowledge.

There are quite tricky decisions here. A current theme is to have IT experience on the board. But what does that actually mean? Building software, running data centres, defending against cyber attack, managing networks? There is also the specialist NED problem. One who cannot contribute on the board outside the specialism. Added to which is the temptation amongst other NEDs, that of downing tools and looking to the specialist NED when the specialism is on the agenda.

I've used IT as an example but any specialism applies. The Chair needs NEDs able to contribute broadly. Sometimes the best answer is to have an advisory group. One that is able to bring specialism to the NEDs independent of the executive.

Another important point is that the Chair and NEDs decide what the tenure of the CEO is likely to be. I don't mean a decision of precisely which date. But a sensible view of whether the CEO will want to go on for several years or wishes to, or ought to go sooner. The importance is in making sure this crucial changeover is under control. It is not for instance allowed to coincide with other key departures such as the Chair. There is usually a clear idea of when a Chair will retire. Knowing this ought to fix the answer to one question. Will this Chair recruit the next CEO or will that be down to a future Chair?

The problem with the succession plan is twofold. Firstly it involves tricky personal discussions. Exacerbated if an individual does not want to leave. Secondly, it is box 2. Important but not urgent. Because it isn't urgent it can get shunted, easier to do nothing than something.

These difficult discussions are also part and parcel of our communications driver. If there is not clarity about succession then mayhem can ensue. There are plenty of examples of NEDs thinking of themselves as the next Chair. Chaos then ensues when the announcement is made and they learn they are not.

Succession planning must also build on the knowledge that

diversity improves corporate performance. There is plenty of research to support this:

> ... *racial diversity is associated with increased sales revenue, more customers, greater market share, and greater relative profits. Gender diversity is associated with increased sales revenue, more customers, and greater relative profits*[1].

However, better results do not always follow because the board is diverse. This is because diversity can only thrive in an inclusive atmosphere. If say key decisions are not taken in board meetings but by a non-diverse sub group of directors in private. Then the lack of inclusion neutralises the diversity and any positive impact. This diversity is seen for what it is, tokenism.

Returning to our earlier theme of design and effectiveness. Chairs need to grasp that diversity is design and inclusion is effectiveness. Decision making will only improve if diversity is included.

Through the succession plan Chairs should consider all aspects of diversity. The visibility of gender, ethnicity and age is obvious. Diversity of experience and education and some disabilities, being 'invisible', can be overlooked. There is a danger of groupthink if everyone has the same education and experience.

The reason for NEDs having fixed terms is to make sure a refresh of board thinking is ongoing. The danger of groupthink being very well known. This regular refresh is a major responsibility of the Chair. It is a great opportunity to refresh thinking, experience and diversity.

Finally, I'd like to return to board effectiveness.

The board is a small group of people led by the Chair and it is largely the Chair who determines its effectiveness. If there is discord, game playing or infighting it is the Chair's role to lead the board out of this. It may need difficult decisions. If the CEO needs wise counsel then this is surely so for the Chair. The advantage to a Chair of a cohesive collegiate group of NEDs is, I hope, obvious. From this will flow support for the Chair, collegiate executives and better decisions.

On the effectiveness of the board effectiveness review. This is down to the quality of the Chair. If the Chair responds to and wants feedback the review will be good. It will be deliberated on by the board and improvements acted on. This is unsurprising, the most effective people want and respond to personal feedback. A weak Chair in comparison is likely to obfuscate, dodge and most of all, pretend.

In conclusion, the Chair has a massive leadership contribution to make. It is far from ceremonial, and fundamentally impacts the culture of the firm.

Edgar Schein is a remarkable source of knowledge about leadership and culture his words are a great conclusion:

*The bottom line for leaders is that if they do not become conscious of the cultures in which they are embedded, those cultures will manage them. Cultural understanding is desirable for all of us, but it is essential to leaders if they are to lead.*[2]

1. Does Diversity Pay?: Race, Gender, and the Business Case for Diversity— First Published April 1, 2009 Research Article Cedric Herring, Department of Sociology—(MC 312), University of Illinois at Chicago
2. Organizational Culture and Leadership (The Jossey-Bass Business & Management Series) By: Edgar H. Schein

# 50

# EPILOGUE

G iven the genesis of this book was a combative NED, what have we discovered?

We have found a commonality between failing boards in four sectors: banks, insurers, hospitals and charities. The implication that this commonality cuts across all other sectors should not be lost. And, we have found key themes.

Firstly, principal-agent is alive and well. It can drive executives to capture an organisation for their own ends and it can also prevent NEDs providing a healthy degree of oversight, support and challenge.

Secondly, the board is not an object or thing. It is a group of people who will either collaborate to make great decisions or, for many and varied reasons, won't. The leadership ability of the Chair to create the environment for non-executives and executives to thrive together is paramount.

And thirdly, I hope you agree we can disagree with my combative NED.

It is possible for NEDs to know what is going on in a large organisation, but only if NEDs take a path less trod. This means two things: firstly, dismissing the idea that spending more time in a business turns a non-executive into an executive and, secondly: getting out there and actually spending more time in the business.

This is only going to work if you go back to my second point above. That the Chair of the Board sees this as the best way to raise the quality of the board's important judgements.

Peter Drucker's words are, on analysis, a statement of the obvious: *"... an effective decision is always a judgement based on "dissenting opinions" rather than a "consensus of the facts."*

It's so obvious because of the answer to another question. What happens to an organisation whose important judgments are poor?

I hope I have also helped you understand culture with its important start point of *Purpose*. And, the all important drivers of behaviour: trust, communication, decision making and incentives. Remember that behaviour is to culture as influence is to leadership. So, when asked to lead a culture change you now know your mission is to influence a change in behaviour.

Finally, it would be great for us to learn from history, but as I said at the outset this is not something we appear to do well. There is nothing I have found and written in this book that someone, somewhere will not read and say: 'well that's hardly a new idea'. To which I reply, if one of the ideas in this book improves one judgement that one board makes, then for me it's been well worth the effort.

Most of all my message to NEDs is to remember what Bagehot wrote nearly a century and a half ago, that cracking shorthand for the role of the NED. You are there to ensure general wisdom:

> *There is in all ordinary joint stock companies a fixed executive*
> *specially skilled, and a somewhat varying council not specially*

*skilled. The fixed manager ensures continuity and experience in the management, and a good board of directors ensures general wisdom.*[1]

---

1. Lombard Street : a description of the money market by Walter Bagehot —1873

# ACKNOWLEDGMENTS

I have been helped and encouraged by a few people whilst writing this book.

Paul Gilbert, CEO of LBC WiseCouncil who kept me writing and without whose faith this book would reside in my mind not in print. Also, my fellow Fellows at the Leadership Centre at Exeter University. Particularly Alan Hooper, founder of the centre and ex-Commandant of the Royal Marines training establishment at Lympstone who inspired my interest in leadership.

Other mentions go to Justin Featherstone MC, a fellow Fellow, and Andy Griffiths OBE: their exploits in Iraq and Afghanistan leave me in awe of what the human spirit is capable.

To all my colleagues at Nationwide, the Bank of England, PRA and FCA, you have taught me more than you will ever know.

My final thanks to Andrew Bailey, who saw through the worst job interview of my entire career to give me a job at the Bank of England. The experience has been amazing.

# ABOUT THE AUTHOR

*John Sutherland is a commercial business leader combining a varied 35 year career in retail banking with eight years at both the FCA and PRA and a year supporting the Parliamentary Commission on Banking Standards.*

During his retail banking career John led sales, marketing, technology, payment services and multi-site back office operations. As a regulator he has worked for the Bank of England, the old FSA and then then the PRA and FCA. This unique combination of business and regulation enables him to bring a different insight to the challenges faced by Non-Executives and Trustees.

A regular speaker on the subject of leadership and governance this is John's first book.

Lightning Source UK Ltd.
Milton Keynes UK
UKHW020653051121
393433UK00006B/42